PRAISE FOR
The Power of Respect

"Aretha Franklin has nothing on Deborah Norville when it comes to understanding the power and importance of respect. I recommend this book to anyone who wants to do anything with anyone else."

— Dick Parsons
Chairman, Citigroup; and
Former Chairman and CEO,
Time Warner

"Deborah Norville reminds us all of what is *really* important in life. The principles in this book *work*! If you want to be happy and healthy and change your life for the better, READ THIS BOOK!"

— Sean Hannity
FOX News

"In her terrific new book, Deborah Norville proves that respect never goes out of style. It offers a fresh take on a simple but powerful truth: treating others well is the cornerstone of good business and a good life."

— Leonard A. Lauder
Chairman Emeritus, The Estée
Lauder Companies, Inc.

"This book could not be more timely! Deborah Norville reminds us of the crucial importance of respect in everyday life and why everyone wins when we treat others—and ourselves—respectfully. *The Power of Respect* should be required reading at home; in businesses, schools, and nonprofit organizations; and in leadership-training programs. In short, every relationship will benefit from the insights contained in Ms. Norville's valuable book."

— Bruce Weinstein, PhD
The Ethics Guy® and Author,
*Is It Still Cheating If I Don't Get
Caught?*

"Deborah Norville is the perfect person to explore respect in this inspiring and practical book. With scientific research, she proves that valuing ourselves and each other is not only important but vital to a strong life."

— Marcus Buckingham
New York Times Best-Selling
Author, *Now, Discover Your
Strengths*

"Deborah Norville uses respect to build integrity into our relationships and honor into our lives."

— Mehmet Oz, MD
New York Times Best-Selling
Author, The *You* Series

"It's the one commodity with zero cost and unlimited gain. It won't shrink your wallet or reduce your list of friends. It's *respect*. And as Deborah Norville skillfully reminds us, practicing the power of respect could quite possibly improve the course of society. Thanks, Deborah, for this insightful study. Count me in!"

— Max Lucado
Pastor and Best-Selling Author

"Just what the doctor ordered! Respect means consideration of others, and Deborah Norville makes a powerful and respectful case as to why we would enrich our own lives and of those around us by making a more conscious effort to live up to this 'forgotten' element of living."

— Steve Forbes
President and CEO,
Forbes Magazine

"The foundation of every relationship, whether at home or work, is respect. If you don't respect the people in your life, then you'll never become someone they can respect. In *The Power of Respect*, Deborah Norville shines a spotlight on our self-focused society and reminds us of the life-changing power of valuing other people above ourselves."

— Dave Ramsey
Radio Talk Show Host;
Best-Selling Author; and FOX
Business Network Host, *The Dave Ramsey Show*

"It is impossible to achieve self-respect, respect for others, or respect from others until each one of us is willing to hold ourselves accountable for our own choices and actions. We have become a blaming society, and as such, Deborah Norville's book could not be more timely for a nation in need of healing on all fronts."

— Christy K. Mack
Cofounder and President,
The Bravewell Collaborative

"*The Power of Respect* radiates a warm glow of human dignity. In an age when basic values are easily overwhelmed by the frenetic pace of events seemingly larger than ourselves, it is vital to remember core truths of human fulfillment. In this charming and graceful book, Deborah Norville reminds us that respect for others is a key to self-respect as well as to personal accomplishment."

— Philip K. Howard
Chairman, Common Good;
and Author, *Life Without Lawyers*

"The Power of Respect identifies a critically important element of individual success. When applied together with other individuals, the culture of mutual respect activates the acceptance of leadership and the empowerment of collaborative innovation for the future."

— Richard E. Caruso, PhD
Founder and Chairman,
Integra LifeSciences and
Uncommon Individual
Foundation

"Deborah Norville's *The Power of Respect* is a beautifully written, old-school lesson for a new generation about the life-changing value of respect. It's a great how-to handbook for parents, couples, students, and all of us in the workplace. It should be a part of the book collection of anyone who is committed to living a full and successful life."

— Byron Pitts
CBS News

"Respect requires giving people the grace to be heard and the warmth of being understood. You don't have to forfeit your identity, ideals, or ideology to have it, just your hostility! Bravo, Deborah Norville, for returning civility to our discourse and respect to our ever increasingly diverse world."

— Bishop T. D. Jakes
Dallas, Texas

"Deborah Norville reminds us that respect is one of the underestimated powers of life. She is a wonder, and so is this book. Both give wise, practical counsel that will immediately help you in friendships and life—at work, school, and play. Deborah's writing is smart, useful, and passionate. Read it, enjoy, and learn the difference it can make in your life."

— Dan Rather
Global Correspondent
and Managing Editor,
Dan Rather Reports, HDNet

The

POWER *of*
RESPECT

The
POWER *of*
RESPECT

Benefit from the
Most Forgotten Element of Success

DEBORAH NORVILLE

THOMAS NELSON
Since 1798

NASHVILLE   DALLAS   MEXICO CITY   RIO DE JANEIRO   BEIJING

Published in Nashville, Tennessee, by Thomas Nelson. Thomas Nelson is a registered trademark of Thomas Nelson, Inc.

Thomas Nelson, Inc. titles may be purchased in bulk for educational, business, fund-raising, or sales promotional use. For information, please e-mail SpecialMarkets@ThomasNelson.com.

Unless otherwise noted, Scripture quotations are taken from the New King James Version®. © 1982 by Thomas Nelson, Inc. Used by permission. All rights reserved.

Scripture quotations marked NCV are from the New Century Version®. © 2005 by Thomas Nelson, Inc. Used by permission. All rights reserved.

Library of Congress Cataloging-in-Publication Data

Norville, Deborah.
    The power of respect: benefit from the most forgotten element of success / Deborah Norville.
      p. cm.
    Includes bibliographical references.
    ISBN 978-0-7852-2760-1 (hardcover)
    1. Respect. 2. Success. I. Title.
BJ1533.R4N67 2009
179'.9—dc22   2009024965

Printed in the United States of America

09 10 11 12 13 QW 5 4 3 2 1

For those who cross the finish line that matters
by letting others go first
and
those who know that
we rise higher when we let others shine.

Human behavior is a fascinating thing to observe. Change your tone of voice or alter your body language, and you can totally change the way another person reacts.

Try it. Reply to someone in a series of short, curt responses, and you'll witness their transformation from calm and blasé to cranky and irritable. But the reverse works too. You've probably noticed the service is a little more solicitous when you're friendly to the waitress. Could a kind word or gesture result in more than just speedy service?

Yes!

If you want to get ahead in your job or get more out of your workers . . .

If you want harmony at home or congeniality at the office . . .

If you want to minimize the possibility of legal action . . .

If you'd just like the world to be a more civil place . . .

If you want to be more creative and more confident . . .

You might be surprised at how all these things and more can be accomplished through one powerful concept:

RESPECT

Contents

Acknowledgments

I had no idea how rich a topic I was exploring when I first began this project. Though it costs absolutely nothing, respect may be one of the most valuable tools any of us can use to achieve our own goals or to help others do the same. It truly is the grease that lubricates the wheels of society—a bit more of it and we might lessen some of the headline-making problems of the world. I am deeply indebted to those researchers and academicians whose studies on the relationship of human interactions have made it possible for me to state with authority the many ways this can be achieved. One professor expressed his frustration that too often their illuminating findings remain buried in dusty academic journals. I am honored to bring a bit of light to the affirmative work being done by so many gifted investigators.

I am lucky to have the advice and friendship of my literary agents at Dupree-Miller, Jan Miller and Shannon Marven, the most dynamic duo in publishing. Ours has been a partnership for many years, and I hope it never ends. I also gratefully acknowledge the team I have been privileged to work with again at Thomas Nelson Publishers. Debbie Wickwire immediately understood the concept of this book, and her sharp editorial intellect added greatly, every step of the way. It is equaled by her sensitivity to the realities of life. Her understanding of the author's challenge of trying to meet publishing deadlines while juggling a full-time job, two school application processes, and other family responsibilities was a godsend. Jennifer Stair's editorial guidance was a welcome addition to the project. Her fresh set of eyes and careful reading of this material was invaluable at a critical juncture. Paula Major also contributed greatly with her assistance as the project neared completion. I hope we all get to collaborate on more projects going forward.

This book began with enormous amounts of research. Hearty thanks and appreciation to Nina Endrst. Her guidance in helping me access the databases I relied upon for initial and follow-up research was hugely important. Many of my observations of how disrespect has permeated our society are made as I am anchoring my daily TV show. I am grateful for my colleagues at *Inside Edition* who day in and day out do such outstanding work. Too often our time-pressured television world doesn't permit the proper amount of appreciation to go their way, and I want to acknowledge their work and that of others at CBS Domestic Television Division.

The Power of Respect begins at home, and certainly that is where I first learned it. To my father, Zack Norville, and my late mother, Merle Olson Norville, thank you for insisting on respect in our home and for teaching your children how to find it in themselves.

It is a lesson I have tried to pass along to my own family, which receives my final acknowledgment. To my husband, Karl, huge thanks for putting up with what proved to be a literary process that usurped far more family time than I ever intended. The way you weave concern for others into both your business and personal affairs is a model for me and so many others. To my children, Niki, Kyle, and Mikaela, the many moments when you've shown special mindfulness for others has lifted my heart even higher than you already do on a daily basis (though I *did* think it was kind of disrespectful to roar through my tiny office with power drills as you installed an Internet line while I was trying to finish this book!).

Finally, I thank God for the curiosity He has given me and the energy to act on it. I know You have me here for a purpose, and I hope this book, in part, helps to fulfill it.

1

The Most Forgotten Element of Success

The Power of Respect

The test had been announced in advance, which meant the students had the chance to study and come to class well prepared. Test papers were handed out, and the college exam commenced. The room was silent, except for the scratching of pencils and the occasional tapping as a student tried to figure out an answer. Until the last question. One by one, as students reached the end of the test, they read the final question with consternation. Some grunted in disgust. One student exclaimed, "You're kidding, right?" Another asked, "Does the last question count toward our grade?" It had to be a joke.

"Yes, it does," replied the teacher, somewhat tersely.

When all the papers were handed in, the professor finally explained. The last question was, "What is the first name of the man who cleans our school?" Virtually every student had been stumped. All of them saw him almost every day. But his *name*? If kids spoke to him, it was usually "Hey, dude." Few students knew his name was Otis.

The professor told the class, "As you go forward in life, you will meet many people. *All* of them are important. No matter what their

1

position, everyone you cross paths with deserves your attention and respect, even if all you do is just smile and say hello. Especially the people you see every day."

I heard that story years ago, and its impact has stayed with me. No one is too unimportant to be ignored. No one is so significant that others don't matter.

Do unto Others . . .

It's a ridiculously simple concept and the first step in the Power of Respect: acknowledging the existence of another person. We all can rattle off a dozen platitudes about it. Walk a mile in their moccasins. The Golden Rule—"Do unto others as you would have them do unto you."[1] Put yourself in their place. Whatever way you say it, when you do it, incredible things can happen.

Doing that brought about an enormous change in Candice Harris's life. She was a young woman in her early twenties, working hard to make it on her own in Atlanta. Growing up, Candice never heard anyone say, "You can do it." She has no recollection of anyone ever encouraging her or pushing her to excel. Candice grew up in a world of lowered expectations. She had never felt she was very important—either at home or at her school. She says her family didn't expect very much of her and made a point of letting her know that. They *actually* said it to her. Candice told me, "It was like, 'This is the extent of what's possible for you.' I felt like it was a good thing if I was small for them."

"You mean like out of the way?" I asked.

"Yeah, like, 'Just keep quiet. Don't make demands. We can only do so much.'" That was especially true when it came to Candice's teeth. They were uneven with huge, noticeable gaps between them. Braces could have solved the problem, but growing up, Candice says she was made to feel she wasn't worthy of them. "My teeth were left that way as a child. Almost like, 'You are not worth the extra dental bills for getting this fixed,'" Candice told me. She continued, "That was even more of a hindrance for my confidence than what my teeth looked like."

Candice paused before she continued. "I never quite believed any of it, or I wouldn't have left home so young." She moved away from home when she was only seventeen and settled in Atlanta two years later. She was a determined young woman, but everything was a struggle. She says it took her a long time to learn some of the basics, like how to rent an apartment or open a bank account. By the time she was twenty-one, she was working as a waitress, dating a not-so-terrific guy, and still hoping to scrape together the money she'd need to get her teeth fixed.

About this same time, Dr. David Garber went out to dinner with some of his business partners at a restaurant in Atlanta. They noticed their waitress, an attractive young woman in her twenties who never seemed to smile, no matter how funny their jokes. When the waitress spoke, they noticed huge gaps between her teeth. Candice was their server. She thought the men were leering at her— like they were "dirty old men." As it happened, her customers were dentists in partnership with Dr. Ronald Goldstein, one of the world's leading innovators in cosmetic dentistry.

The dentists persuaded Candice to come in for a consultation. She was painfully shy about how her smile looked. In fact, she was so shy that it was difficult to get her to even smile so Dr. Goldstein could take dental photos for evaluation. There was no way Candice could afford the kind of dental work that would give her a smile she'd be proud of. In fact, ironically, she had made inquiries just that week about trying to obtain credit to pay for the procedure.

Dr. Goldstein isn't just any dentist. He pioneered many of the techniques in cosmetic dentistry and literally wrote the book on aesthetic dentistry. His scholarly articles have been widely published. But

Dr. Goldstein, who graduated from dental school in 1957, has made a lifelong practice of providing dental treatments to those who can't afford it. He told me, "It's just something in my brain. If I see people who need help, and they can't do it and I can, well, I would lose respect for me if I didn't do that service for them."

Dr. Goldstein and his team, including dual-degree specialist, Dr. Garber, and orthodondist/periodontist and implant world authority, Dr. Maurice Salama, provided their services pro bono. They created porcelain veneers large enough to fill in the gaps in Candice's teeth and reshaped uneven surfaces that marred the teeth on her lower jaw. When the work was finally done, Candice was given a mirror to check out her new smile. She was overwhelmed with emotion. Smiling was no longer a problem. Wiping away tears, she couldn't stop herself from smiling.

For Candice, it was the beginning of monumental change. In the past, every picture of her showed a young woman with sad eyes, smiling with a closed mouth. Now she grinned spontaneously. She started to like herself and took charge of her life. She dumped the lousy boyfriend, enrolled in college, and last December, Candice graduated with a degree in finance and a whole new perspective on what her life could be. Unlike most graduates in the class of 2009, Candice landed a job in a law firm within three months of getting her diploma.

The Power of Respect ignited by a smile.

For Dr. Goldstein, it's all about helping people to like themselves. He told me, "It is very difficult to expect or even demand respect from others if you don't respect yourself. When certain people are so terribly embarrassed to smile because they hate their smile, it can and many times does, start a downward spiral domino effect."

Candice doesn't agree that the changes in her life came just from the difference in her appearance. "I don't think that I support the frame of mind that if you cosmetically fix something it will give you the tools you need. It probably gave me a few more cards in my deck to deal with things, for sure. Maybe I look the part more." The biggest change for Candice is confidence. Confidence that came from the respectful and altruistic acts of people who were strangers.

"When I break it down, having these men do this thing that meant something to them probably made more of a difference than just the cosmetic change. They were just good-hearted men who said, 'We care for you, and we want to see you have a better life.'" Even more, they believed in Candice, something she hadn't always had in her life.

"He had, and to this day, has such high expectations for what's possible for me," Candice says, with a hint of wonder in her voice. "I just don't want to disappoint Dr. Goldstein."

Don't worry, Candice, you haven't.

"She is an amazing, amazing young woman," Dr. Ronald Goldstein gushes. It's been several years since Goldstein and his team reshaped Candice's smile, but he's as excited today about her transformation as he was the moment she first looked in the mirror. In fact, if such a thing is possible, the impact on the man who provided that gorgeous smile might actually be stronger than on the young woman who received it. He says it's all the Power of Respect.

"You have to have a good image of yourself, and if you don't have that, you disrespect yourself and others as well," he explains. "Probably twenty-five hundred studies have proven that beauty and health go together. And every single study we have has shown the effectiveness of looking one's best; you feel good about yourself."

But no one doles out hundreds of thousands of dollars' worth of free dental work just because surveys say appearance is linked to positive self-image. During his fifty-year career, Dr. Goldstein has set up community-based dental programs for the mentally ill. He is the founding donor for Tomorrow's Smiles, a group that provides routine and cosmetic dental care for teens at risk of dropping out of school.

What propels such extraordinary generosity? The answer can be found way back in the anti-Semitic South, in which Ronald

Goldstein grew up. He was a Jewish boy raised in Georgia at a time when the Ku Klux Klan had few reservations about making its presence known. The renowned dentist told me what it was like. "You had to run faster than the others and deal with problems of prejudice. When you have had to deal with adversity, you learn to be tough. You learn how to fight. So I have had to do that."

It was during that period of talking tough just to survive that Goldstein, then just a boy in grammar school, did something that he never forgot. "One of the kids in our school was dying of cancer," he recalled. "We found out the one thing he wanted was a bicycle. Well, that got to me and I did a fund-raiser with those old Blue Horse notebooks. We earned thousands and thousands of coupons for that bicycle. I felt this need to help others, because others had helped me." Goldstein says it may look like he's helping others, but he's helping himself at the same time. "It helps my self-respect and my respect for *me* when I do good for others."

> Management is doing things right; leadership is doing the right things.
> —PETER F. DRUCKER

Talk about the Power of Respect turning things around! It's almost weird how nice some people have become at the lumberyard. Too nice, in fact. One worker there calls the polite and solicitous way one executive interacts "nauseating" because he is so easygoing. The worker went to the boss and asked him to have the executive "tone it down" a bit. The reason this is noteworthy is six months earlier, the nearly sixty-year-old firm was on shaky ground, not because of the tough economy but because of the outrageous way some employees at the building materials company were being treated.

Imagine the shock—and fear—of employees who came to work the Monday before Christmas to find the boss didn't show up and instead left a two-and-a-half-page letter. A letter that began like this:

> I am taking a leave of absence for a month and will not return until January 19, 2009. I am not sure what I am going to do or where I am going, but I will not be here in the office.

The letter went on to refer to an incident the previous week that left one woman so upset she didn't come to work the following day. She was disturbed about the incident and distressed the boss didn't come to her defense. In his letter, the head of the company said he had grown tired of settling disputes and had reached the point where he thought it best if the disagreement just played itself out. The letter continued:

> It was the straw that broke the camel's back. There has been a history around here of people not respecting each other and as of this moment, it's over. It has gotten to the point where I am afraid to even leave the office for fear that people will begin to air their differences. I have been afraid to take even an extended vacation for myself.
>
> Going forward, people are either going to treat each other with respect, dignity, and courtesy or else I will retire. I have worked too hard and too long to watch this company be torn down. I'll get out (and cash out) before I allow that to happen.
>
> YOU WILL treat each other respectfully or else I am leaving.
>
> When I return, I will ask several people in the office whether or not they have been treated more respectfully in my absence. If they have, I will roll up my sleeves and get back to work in earnest. If nothing has changed, I will move on.

Wow. "YOU WILL treat each other respectfully, or else I am leaving." The message, delivered during the low point of the economic crisis, was crystal clear: if you want to keep your job, change the way you treat people at work. But the boss didn't just deliver an ultimatum and leave it at that. His letter also offered simple specifics on what employees could do that would make a positive difference during his thirty-day time-out. He suggested, "Simply say, 'Good morning.' It's not that hard." He referred to the office worker who'd been on the receiving end of abuse. "Ask her if she needs help. Be kind." The company is in the lumber business, but the language around the office was beginning to sound like it was a construction site. "The 'F' word is inexcusable, even though it is common in the construction business. If you have to cuss, do it when I'm not around." Finally, he suggested people simply clean up after themselves, rather than leave their trash for someone else to pick up.

The boss made good on his promise and didn't set foot in the family-owned business for one month. His absence had an impact. He told me, "I think I have opened some eyes in terms of how teamwork can best be achieved, and that begins with each individual valuing each other as individuals." That doesn't sound like a complicated lesson, but the roots of the business can be found on the local docks. The firm originally provided materials to shore up and secure cargo in and out of the port. Early employees were constantly dealing with stevedores and port captains, a testosterone-laden bunch not known much for politeness or consideration. Containerization changed the need for rough lumber on the docks, and the firm developed new product lines. But the coarse culture generated during the dockworker days didn't die easily. The owner's self-imposed sabbatical drove the message home. His weekly paycheck memos make sure the message is regularly received.

During his month away from the business, the man whose father started the business struggled with how he could really communicate the kind of respectful behavior he was hoping to see from his employees. He decided to target where he knew they'd see it: their pay envelope. Every payday since his return, along with each worker's paycheck, he slips a short, one-page memo with an uplifting message into the envelope. He's talked about gossip and gratitude, thinking big and finding a purpose. He thinks these memos are making a difference in the company. "The two greatest commandments in the Bible," he says, "are to love the Lord your God with all your heart, mind, soul, and strength and your neighbor as yourself."[2] He's talked about that in his paycheck memos.

"To love your neighbor, you have to show them respect," he continues. "That's what I am trying to do both by example and by memo." Imagine a business owner who puts such a premium on respect that he was willing to pull the plug on his business if he didn't start seeing more of it at his company. His drastic move worked.

Six months after he made his stand, the lumber company owner told me things had certainly gotten better. The woman who'd been so upset by the way she was treated is back at her job and enjoying interaction with colleagues who are now considerate. Not only is their approach in dealing with her more respectful, he told me, "They are actually going out of their way to see how they might assist her specifically with her responsibilities." Other employees have recognized that not only is she really good at what she does, but her expertise is important to the overall enterprise (and thus *their* bottom lines).

The executive who had others shaking their heads because he'd become so kind is actually something of a role model to his employees. The boss explains, "The whole atmosphere or office dynamic can be markedly improved upon by one person trying to set an example or make a difference." No one has asked him to stop including the memos with their paychecks. The messages are powerful and uplifting. In fact, I've asked to have them e-mailed to me even though I don't work there.

It takes a lot of time to write those memos and work one-on-one to encourage respectful behavior. I asked why he does it. The lumber executive was passionate in his response. "I don't want to hurt people. I am trying to elevate people and help them grow as human beings, to show consideration for others and reach their maximum potential." Those are lessons for life, but the business benefits too. "Changing how we interact through respect not only can be helpful in office dynamics," he continued, "but it also can overlap into school, even nations. One person can make a difference." It all begins with respect.

THE POWER OF RESPECT
Everyone deserves respect.

Successful people know that respect is key to success.

Many superstars and coaches in the sports world know the Power of Respect. When Ryne Sandberg was inducted into the Baseball Hall of Fame in 2005, the former Chicago Cubs second baseman attributed his success to one thing: respect. He said he had too much respect for his coaches and managers not to give it his all every game. Baseball makes stars of super sluggers and big play makers, but Sandberg used his acceptance speech to emphasize his team. He said, "The name on the front [team] is a lot more important than the name on the back [your own]. That's respect."[3]

Legendary UCLA basketball coach John Wooden certainly knew that respect is a key element of success. Accomplishing an unprecedented ten NCAA National Championships and eighty-eight consecutive victories, Coach Wooden insisted on respect from his players. He told them, "Never score without acknowledging a teammate" and "Treat your opponent with respect."[4]

At Oprah Winfrey's Harpo Studios in Chicago, the climate of respect is almost palpable. Years ago, Oprah asked me to come on her show and talk about one of my books. From my first point of contact at the studios—the security man who opened the garage door to let me in—I was enveloped in a wave of appreciation from the staff. "We're so glad you're here," I was greeted by almost everyone.

This level of respect starts at the top. *Black Enterprise* magazine quotes Oprah as saying, "Treating people with respect is

> Treat everyone with politeness, even those who are rude to you—not because they are nice, but because you are.
> —UNKNOWN

the most important thing to me. It's not just talk. I don't yell at people. I don't mistreat people. I don't talk down to people, so no one else in this building, in this vicinity, has the right to do it."[5] That attitude has been behind an impressive record of success that includes a widely popular talk show, radio network, television and film projects, and as of January 2010, a 50 percent stake in Winfrey's own cable television network.

You'll find a similar attitude of respect at Studio 44 in the CBS Broadcast Center, where we tape *Inside Edition*. For the couple of hours (and on days when nothing goes right, a *lot* more!) I spend in there, my experience is truly delightful. How many people can describe even a part of their day at work as delightful? We call ourselves "the studio people." It's not just the team's professionalism that makes our time in the studio delightful, though I know how good my guys are. Wayne, our stage manager, filters through the headset chatter and never fails to give me a heads-up when it looks like a story might suddenly change. Tommy, our stagehand, sees glints of light where they shouldn't be and fixes problems before anyone else even knows about them. Dean has maneuvered two huge cameras at once in a pinch, and I've seen Larry's quick thinking fix a shot and save the show more times than I can count. It is

> Manners are a sensitive awareness of the feelings of others. If you have that awareness, you have good manners, no matter what fork you use.
>
> —EMILY POST

wonderful to work with a team where everyone has each other's back. That is a form of respect.

But what makes my time in the studio delightful is how unfailingly polite everyone is. It's common to hear "Thank you, sir" when a cord gets yanked out of the camera's field of vision. And "My pleasure, my friend" in reply. This consideration of others impacts the tenor of civility in that room. When other cameramen or stagehands fill in on occasion, they joke that they've gotten time off for good behavior. People like to work in Studio 44 because it's a pleasant place.

A FRONT-ROW SEAT

There's a blessing and a curse to having a job like mine at *Inside Edition*. The blessing of anchoring this television news show is that I have a front-row seat for what's happening in the world. Sometimes the stories make your heart swell with pride, like the tale of Jason McElwain, who had the respect and admiration of his school—and the entire nation—when he scored an astonishing twenty points in the last four minutes of the final regular game of the season. Most of the time, Jason was known as "the kid with autism," but on this day, the coach told the seventeen-year-old who served as the team's manager to suit up. Jason had never played in a game before.

Jason was carried off the court on the team's shoulders. Students at the school were clamoring for his autograph. He later got to meet

President George W. Bush. His mom, Debbie, said he was an inspiration for people everywhere with disabilities.[6]

If you're ever in a hospital where the walls are alive with color, where ceiling tiles sport rainbows and butterflies just where a patient on a gurney might see them, chances are John Feight has been there. Feight is a man who embodies the Power of Respect. He has spent the past thirty years traveling the world, painting every hospital surface imaginable with beautiful images that promote healing. It started when he was visiting a sick friend and thought the dreary halls could use a splash of color. One little girl, a burn victim, silently watched him work. When he offered her a brush and suggested she help paint, her smile launched a mission that has taken the healing power of art to hospitals in all but a half dozen nations on earth. The founder of the Foundation for Hospital Art, John Feight believes everyone is an artist.[7] Like a pied piper, he attracts visitors, medical staff, and most importantly patients, who eagerly grab brushes to fill in the murals he's sketched.

Feight looks like a doctor in his paint-splattered green scrubs. He says painting takes patients away from their medical problems into a pain-free world of creativity. He learned just how transformative that process could be when he was treated for prostate cancer. As soon as Feight was well enough, he went back to the hospital where he had been treated and painted the bare ceiling he'd stared at during his stay.[8]

The story of Patrick Henry Hughes is another touching reminder that all of us have something unique. Patrick Henry Hughes is just more unique than most. Born blind, with multiple physical disabilities, Patrick Henry has been in a wheelchair his whole life. What he lacks in physical abilities, he more than compensates for in musical talent. His fingers fly over the piano and his voice is clear and strong, creating music that demands that you stop and drink in the sound.

When the University of Louisville marching band hits the field, you can't miss Patrick. That's right—he's the trumpet player in the wheelchair, being maneuvered around by his father. It is a beautiful story of love and respect. His father learns the marching band's routine so he doesn't miss a step during halftime. The elder Mr. Hughes, who's also named Patrick, can also be found in the classrooms at U of L, guiding his son from class to class. He works the overnight shift in order to be available for his son. Mr. Hughes said he never felt he was sacrificing anything for his son. On the contrary, he said, "It's what Patrick does for me." You can't help but watch the Hugheses' incredible story and marvel at the father-son bond as well as feel yourself drawn closer to the loved ones in your own life.[9]

I've loved seeing these stories on *Inside Edition,* but the flip side of my job is that I see other stories all too close up. Lately the picture isn't very pretty.

There was the cute little cheerleader who thought she was going to a sleepover. Instead she was jumped by her so-called friends, who then proceeded to videotape the attack. The horrible girls proved their stupidity by posting the episode online—enabling the rest of the world to learn of their vicious acts and helping cops to make multiple arrests. Victoria Lindsay was left with a concussion and hearing and vision loss. Her attackers were left with criminal records. They were sentenced to probation.[10]

Did you see the fourteen-year-old kid in Baltimore who got reamed out by the police officer for riding his skateboard where he wasn't supposed to? It was no wonder. It was obvious to everyone (and everyone saw it because the video ended up on YouTube) that young Eric just could not stop himself from saying "dude" to the officer. Officer Rivieri was *not* amused.[11]

It is ridiculous that anyone would call 911 to complain that the local McDonald's didn't have the Chicken McNuggets she ordered.

(Yes, that *really* happened—in Fort Pierce, Florida.) LaTreasa Goodman told cops she wouldn't have made a stink if the cashier taking her order had told her in advance the restaurant was out of McNuggets.[12]

Downright tragic is the only way to describe what happened in DeKalb County, Georgia, where eleven-year-old Jaheem Herrera hanged himself last April. His friend said, "He's tired of everybody always messing with him at school."[13] The boy was the object of "relentless bullying" at his elementary school. His little sister discovered his body.

Outrageous is the adjective that comes to mind in the Thomas Junta story. He's currently serving a six- to ten-year prison sentence for killing a man in Massachusetts during a kids' hockey practice. Junta complained the victim's kids were playing too aggressively. They exchanged words, then Junta beat the man. The children were watching.[14] Junta has twice been denied parole.

We all have our favorite songs, but can you imagine killing a man over a Jimmy Buffett song? Neither can I—but it happened. A soldier from Fort Bragg died after a fight outside a bar in Steamboat Springs, Colorado, last January. Well, it wasn't really even a fight. Richard Lopez had selected a Jimmy Buffett song on the jukebox and some other patrons heckled him about the choice. Later, when Lopez and his friends left the bar, one of the hecklers punched Lopez in the face and his head hit the pavement. He never regained consciousness. Several eyewitnesses say Lopez never raised a hand toward his assailant.[15]

> Without feelings of respect, what is there to distinguish men from beasts?
>
> —CONFUCIUS

From Hollywood starlets to Wall Street moguls (and many people in between), it is becoming far more common for the headlines to highlight people with disrespectful attitudes and behaviors.

I used to think that people eventually get around to doing the right thing because, well, it's the right thing to do. Yet after years of reporting stories of violence, rudeness, and disrespect, I now realize that may not be the case for everyone.

Frustration about how humans interact is nothing new. Since the time of Confucius, more than two thousand years ago, people have behaved obnoxiously enough to warrant concern.

Excuuuse Me—Must We Be So Rude?

Americans don't often agree on many things, but when it comes to respect, people say there's less of it lately. Nearly eight in ten Americans (79 percent) say a lack of respect and courtesy is a serious national problem, and most people say it's getting worse (60 percent). Seventy-three percent say we used to treat one another with greater respect. When asked if they felt that way because of "a false nostalgia for a past that never existed," only 21 percent said yes.[16] The rest of us think that Americans' attitude of disrespect really is worse these days.

Rudeness in America

- 79 percent say lack of respect is a serious problem.
- 60 percent say rude and selfish behavior is increasing.
- 88 percent sometimes encounter rude people.
- 62 percent are bothered by rude behavior.
- 77 percent see clerks ignoring customers.
- 58 percent encounter aggressive drivers.
- 56 percent are bothered by foul language.[17]

What has people feeling this way? The list is long and touches on almost every aspect of daily life. Get cut off by someone on the highway? In a 2002 survey conducted by Public Agenda, aggressive driving topped the list of "aggravating circumstances." Fifty-eight percent of survey respondents say they are confronted by reckless and aggressive drivers, and nearly two-thirds believe it's getting worse. One lady who 'fessed up to being aggressive behind the wheel (and 35 percent admit they're guilty of aggressive driving) said the car was like a cocoon, separating you from the other drivers and providing a sense of anonymity. It's easy to act like a jerk when you feel no connection to the folks around you.[18]

Sideline screamers also made the list. Out-of-control parents at youth sports events who shout at coaches, referees, and the kids are not just getting on the nerves of the person being yelled at. In the Public Agenda survey, 71 percent of people who watch organized sports for kids say they've seen sideline screamers, and two-thirds are bothered by them.

> I get no respect.
> —RODNEY DANGERFIELD

Loud cell phone use, calls in inappropriate places, crude language on the Internet or in conversation, surly staff at stores, and those interminable waits on customer "service" lines at companies also ranked high on the list of aggravations.[19]

WHAT IS RESPECT?

What exactly is respect? Thanks to Aretha Franklin, we all know how to spell it. Her strong, powerful rendition of the song "Respect" makes listeners sit a bit straighter, walk a bit taller, and be a bit more self-assured. But Aretha singing about respect did something more: it inspired us to *expect* respect from others.

The song was written by Otis Redding, but under Aretha its message took on a life of its own. Jerry Wexler, who influenced the careers of stars like Ray Charles, Bob Dylan, and the Drifters, produced many of Franklin's hits, including "Respect." He told *Rolling Stone* magazine the song was "global in its influence, with overtones of the civil-rights movement and gender equality. It was an appeal for dignity."[20]

With Aretha Franklin at the microphone, the song "Respect" became an anthem for anyone who'd felt diminished and disrespected—and there were plenty of them in 1967 when the song topped the charts. Listen carefully to the song, and you'll hear that it is really a command. You better find out what *I* consider respect to be.

Discover what *someone else* calls respect. *That* is the key to the Power of Respect. While there are some generally agreed-upon ideas of what respect is, at its heart, the definition of respect is different for everyone. In this book, you will discover ways to find out what respect means to you and experience the Power of Respect in your own life.

The dictionary defines *respect* as "To feel or show deferential regard for; esteem."[21] My own definition after having spent so much time exploring respect is "Acknowledging the value and uniqueness of others and being mindful of their feelings, while at the same time trying to put myself in their position."

The word itself comes from the Latin *respectus,* which means "regard." Break it down further—*re-,* meaning "back," and *specere,* meaning "look at"—and we can understand why respect is such a potent force. It all comes down to how you "look back at" yourself and others.

THE POWER OF RESPECT

Respect is how you "look back at" yourself and others.

Self-respect is a critical component of success. Your sense of self-respect is dictated by how you "look back at" yourself and is largely determined by your sense of self-worth. *Am I reaching my potential? Am I living my life as I should? Am I pleased with the choices I have made and the direction my life is taking? Am I caring for my health? Am I nourishing my intellect? Am I where I want to be on my spiritual journey?* These are some of the default checks made when measuring your self-respect. Notice they all are areas of your life over which you have control.

Respect is also about how others "look back at" us. We cannot control how others regard us. We can only determine our standing among others by the cues we perceive. *Am I greeted with enthusiasm (or not at all)? Am I picked for the team? Is my opinion solicited (and if so, acted upon)? Am I invited to the party? Am I being made to wait longer than that other customer? Is my boss abrupt with me?* We constantly ask these questions and process our perceptions of daily interactions. These help us intuit where we rank in the social hierarchy. The more intimate the relationship and the person's impact on our life, the more importance we attach to how we perceive his or her response.

> There are two things people want more than sex and money . . . recognition and praise.
> —MARY KAY ASH

Respect requires empathy, the capacity to anticipate and understand the feelings of others. It requires consideration. It is letting the Golden Rule shape the way we interact. It's being mindful to see a situation from another's perspective. When respect is given, it communicates to the recipient of the respect that he is valued and important. That unleashes the Power of Respect: the goodwill generated boomerangs back to the giver in the form of loyalty, trust, and mutual respect.

THE POWER OF RESPECT
CAN MAKE A DIFFERENCE

Would you like to experience the Power of Respect in your own life? Before we go on, consider a few questions:

- Do you wish your children were more polite?
- Do you feel as though you are really sharing your marriage, or just coexisting with your spouse?
- Have you ever been treated rudely by a friend?
- Would you like to have more friends and truly feel a part of a positive, enriching community?
- If you are a teacher, are you convinced you could really help your students if you didn't have to spend so much time trying to keep them quiet?
- Or as a teacher, do you wish your class had higher academic achievement?
- If you are a student, would you like to learn but think since your classroom is like a zoo, you can't?
- Are you a business owner who'd like to save time and money by not having to train new employees as often?
- Are you a retailer wondering why the amount you're ringing up in sales doesn't seem consistent with the amount of foot traffic in your shop?
- Would you like to reduce your firm's potential exposure to lawsuits?
- Do you wish people would treat you with more respect?

- Would you like to feel valuable and important, no matter what your circumstances may be?
- Could you be more successful in life if only you had more confidence and self-respect?

Chances are you answered yes to several of those questions. And though there are many underlying causes to these problems, the solutions have one common theme—the Power of Respect!

Across America, there is a general sense that people are not as nice as they used to be. Remember, 79 percent of us think a lack of respect and courtesy is a big problem.[22] What's happening in the outside world seems to be spilling over into schools, where 73 percent of teachers and 68 percent of parents believe kids absorb the disrespect that is rampant in our culture and bring it with them to class.[23] It's costing businesses in lost productivity as employees who feel unimportant decrease their work effort or, worse, leave to find jobs where they do feel valued. It's impacting our relationships, where those forgotten niceties create divides that widen into irreparable breaches.

At this writing, America is in the worst economic crisis in more than a generation. A return to civility will not immediately thaw the freeze in credit or restore decimated 401(k)s. A new climate of respect will not create new jobs, nor will it turn Ponzi schemers of the Bernie Madoff ilk into law-abiding citizens.

The Power of Respect, however, can make a difference.

The Power of Respect can keep families intact. Kids who learn to respect their parents, and are in turn shown respect by their parents, are more likely to succeed in life than kids who did not have respect taught and modeled in the home.

The Power of Respect can keep marriages together. In the majority of lasting marriages, both spouses say the respect they have for each other has been an essential component in their partnership.

The Power of Respect can save lives. In a new epidemic in America, called "bullycide," an increasing number of kids kill themselves every year, no longer able to endure the taunts and harassment of bullies. The Power of Respect can restore relationships, create an atmosphere where friendships thrive, and inspire people to give more of themselves to others.

The Power of Respect can restore calm to our classrooms. It can enable students to learn more and score higher on achievement tests, where lately America is falling woefully behind.

The Power of Respect can save American businesses an estimated sixty-four billion dollars. That's the estimated cost of losing and replacing professionals and managers who quit their jobs because of perceived workplace unfairness. That staggering figure is equivalent to the gross domestic product of the fifty-five wealthiest countries in the world![24]

The Power of Respect can increase effectiveness of leaders in every area of life by elevating respect for authority and increasing the likelihood that people will respond to their leadership in a positive way.

The Power of Respect can foster individual achievement through self-respect. Feeling valued by others bolsters confidence and inspires creativity. Individuals, once tentative and hesitant, will find the courage to push the boundaries and accomplish new goals.

THE POWER OF RESPECT
The Power of Respect can make a difference.

PROOF OF THE POWER OF RESPECT

How can I state with such certainty that the Power of Respect can make a difference? Because there is proof. For the past two years, I have been trolling academic literature looking for evidence that measurable benefits could be attributed to more respectful, civil interactions between individuals. In my previous book, *Thank You Power,* I pointed out the connection between the practice of gratitude and positive measurable outcomes, including better health, improved cognitive skills, greater resilience, and a more positive outlook.[25] As an "others-focused" emotion, Thank You Power shifts the emphasis from yourself to another individual, with impressive benefits coming back to your-self. This boomerang effect of putting the concerns of others ahead of your own has been shown to yield unexpected but welcome payback to the giver.

> Coming together is a beginning. Keeping together is progress. Working together is success.
> —HENRY FORD

The Power of Respect works in a similar way. As you will see in the chapters that follow, the others-focused aspect of the Power of Respect elevates the recipients of respect, causing them to operate at higher performance. Whether you are a parent wanting to teach your children to be responsible family members, a business leader trying to increase worker productivity, or a schoolteacher eager for your students to learn, the benefits of respect actually return to you in the form of improved relationships and increased effectiveness in your pursuits.

Successful people know that no one climbs the tallest mountains alone. The view from the top is always sweeter when shared with someone else. The Power of Respect not only will assure that you reach your goals, but it also will assure that many friends and loved ones will be there cheering when you do.

Respect Reminders

--- ⌗ ---

- ☐ Being respectful to others makes them feel valued.
- ☐ Respectful people are trusted.
- ☐ Respect fosters "connectedness" which leads to:
  - Stronger personal relationships.
  - Greater employee loyalty.
  - Higher customer sales.
  - Improvements in education.
  - Greater creativity.

2

It All Starts at Home

The Power of Respect at Home

"I don't care, I *want* it!" The loud, insistent voice of the willful child filled the grocery store aisle, heading into shrill.

"But we're not buying more candy today. You already picked out a bag," the weary mother said, reaching to take the sack of chocolates from her son's hand. He looked to be seven, maybe eight years of age. Far too old for this kind of scene in a grocery store.

"No!" he shouted. "I want *this* candy, and you can't stop me, you stupid mom!" Several heads turned, and one woman's mouth dropped at the scene.

"Oh, Jeremy, honestly." The mother, defeated, flipped the bag into the shopping cart. "You are impossible."

A variation of this scene happens every day in virtually every community of America. We've all seen it: spoiled, willful children whose parents seem defeated and overwhelmed. Kids who seem to have the upper hand.

Sadly, many of them don't grow out of it. How would you respond to a teenage guest in your home who, when reminded of the rules on curfew, looks you straight in the eye and says, "If I don't make it home by then, there's nothing you could do about it"? I don't know who was more shocked: the hostess or her dinner guests who were within earshot.

> Discipline doesn't break a child's spirit half as often as the lack of it breaks a parent's heart.
>
> —UNKNOWN

More than one parent could identify with the frazzled New York mother who'd had it with her squabbling daughters. She did what many a parent has threatened. She pulled the car over in a suburban neighborhood and left the girls by the side of the road. The real-life incident mirrored a plotline from the television show *Desperate Housewives* and made headlines around the world. When police found the mom, a successful attorney, she was arrested. Child endangerment charges were later dropped.[1]

Report on Civility

- 89 percent say incivility is a serious problem today.
- 90 percent of those same people said they were not personally rude.
- 50 percent say incivility is extremely serious.
- 78 percent said civility has deteriorated considerably over the past ten years.
- 90 percent believe incivility contributes to the increasing violence.
- 85 percent believe incivility divides the national community.
- 85 percent believe incivility erodes crucial values such as respect.[2]

There is a sense that children today are much more willful and quick to backtalk. If that's true, it may be that children are simply mirroring the world they live in.

It isn't anything new. Even the Pilgrims must have had problems with their kids. A law passed in 1641 in the Commonwealth of Massachusetts made it illegal for anyone under the age of sixteen to "smite" their parents.

Yale law professor Stephen Carter has written extensively on the lack of civility in America. He defines *civility* as "the sum of all the sacrifices we make for the sake of living together. The sense of going the extra mile, doing something we don't have to do that the law doesn't require in order to make someone else's life a little bit better."[3] Professor Carter believes one of the reasons for growing incivility is that children are not learning to behave. Perhaps that's because parents aren't sure how to teach them. Corny as it sounds, it begins with "please" and "thank you." The Power of Respect in its infancy is politeness. Like many positive behaviors, minding your manners begins at home.

THE POWER OF RESPECT
The Power of Respect begins at home.

FIVE SIMPLE STEPS
TO RAISING RESPECTFUL KIDS

Every expert on human behavior knows that people continue the behaviors that get noticed. This immutable fact of human behavior is key to combating the growing incivility and lack of respect. The other critical fact of human behavior is that we do best the things we are taught. Whether it's writing our name, playing an instrument, making our beds, or any of the other things we know how to do, we are better at it when someone shows us how to do it correctly. Parents make a point of teaching many skills to their youngsters and begin the education early. But respect? How do we go about teaching our children to be polite and respectful?

The answer, it turns out, can be found in five simple steps. You read right: simple. These five guidelines serve as a framework for building respect, no matter what age the child.

How to Raise Respectful Kids

1. **Be with your kids.** Spend time with your kids and listen to them—with no agenda. Just be together.
2. **Praise the positive.** When your kids behave the way you want them to (the way they are *supposed* to), make sure you let them know you noticed.
3. **Ignore the negative.** This is the hard one: it will nearly do you in to *not* speak about what they are doing to annoy you. But this is essential to teaching proper behavior.
4. **Define your rules.** Talk together about your family's rules about honesty, computer/video use, chores. Discuss why the rules are what they are and the consequences of violating them.
5. **Spell out—and act out—respect.** Be clear with your children about your family's traditions and values, and show them what those values look like in action.

BE WITH YOUR CHILD

Being a parent is exhausting. When your kids are toddlers, they wake up way too early and their naps don't last nearly long enough. For a busy mom trying to watch the youngsters, tidy the house, do the laundry and the shopping, and make dinner, it can be a struggle. Factor in a job outside the home, along with the care and feeding of a husband, and it can be overwhelming. The last thing you want to do is sit on the floor with your child and build one more tower with wooden blocks. I can remember being so wiped out when my children were young, I used to pile up the stuffed animals to keep me propped upright when we were building Thomas the Tank Engine trains.

However much I may have wanted to be taking a nap or tidying the house instead, it turns out that time I spent on the floor was helping to raise my children to be respectful individuals.

"As parents, we have to spend time with our kids when there is no task involved," says Dr. Harold Koplewicz, one of the nation's leading child and adolescent psychiatrists and founder of the New York University Child Study Center. He says that "together time" is much more impactful than one would think. "Let them call the shots. If they want to play Candyland two hundred times," he says, "you play it. You don't take phone calls, you don't look at your BlackBerry, and you don't keep the TV on. Focus on your child." An expert in child mental health disorders and child development, Koplewicz talked with me about the role parents can play in bringing up respectful kids. It starts with the one thing we all have so little of— time. So just "be" with your kids. Without all the distractions.

> The best thing to spend on your children is your time.
> —LOUISE HART

THE POWER OF RESPECT

*Set aside time each day to be with your kids,
without distractions.*

"We all want to be validated by others," Dr. Koplewicz said. Kids know how busy we are. Even at young ages, children are aware of Mom and Dad's to-do list. Dr. Koplewicz says whether it's ten minutes or half an hour, those few minutes with your children remind your youngsters that they are valued. Quality time with parents with no particular agenda except to enjoy each other's company reinforces for the child that there is something about him or her that is appealing enough to their parents that they *choose* to be with their child. It helps develop the child's self-respect and emphasizes that home is a safe place. Koplewicz also suggests that together time lays the foundation on which a family's values system and methods of correcting bad behaviors and encouraging good ones can be built.[4]

"A child needs to be listened to and have the right questions asked back," says Dr. Mary Pulido, an expert on social welfare with more than twenty years of experience working with high-risk children and families. "To think, 'I am important, and what I say counts,' and to have that validation that the parent is listening to them does wonders with children."

Dr. Pulido is executive director of the New York Society for the Prevention of Cruelty to Children. Sometimes the Society needs to move mountains in dealing with kids' misbehavior, and therapists have found that parental playtime with children can be an important tool in helping damaged families mend. The Society, the oldest child welfare agency in the country, is a place where children who have been beaten or abused in other ways by family members receive care and counseling, as do their parents, many of whom Dr. Pulido says were abused themselves as children.

Introducing the Power of Respect, though the Society doesn't call it that, is a component of the intense therapy the NYSPCC provides. "The concept of tuning in to your child, respecting your child, and creating optimism in your child is not even on their radar screen," Pulido told me. "Respect, in the parents' minds, is a one-way street where they feel the child needs to respect them. The majority of these parents are repeating behaviors they learned as children. They were not respected. Their voices were not heard." The Society deals with truly fractured families. Most of them are there by court order, mandated to participate in the NYSPCC's sessions.

What looks like playtime is actually serious business. At times, caseworkers have had to actually teach parents *how* to play with their children. How to get down on the floor. How to engage their child. How to let the youngster select what they're going to do. Dr. Pulido says it's a huge undertaking. But eventually, abusers and the little ones they've shattered can slowly begin to heal. As the Society's executive director puts it, "They come here wilted, and we try to help make them bloom again."[5]

"Being" with your children will change as they develop. Playing blocks and building trains with toddlers will morph into playing board games, riding bikes, and building model planes. As children mature into adolescence, they may see their parents as more of a mode of transportation than companions with whom to spend time. Painful as it may be for parents, that separation is a healthy part of a child's development. Shopping trips, trips to the ballpark, or shared tickets to a favorite band's concert are possible bonding opportunities. What you do with your child is not important, as long as it's an activity your child selects and for the time you have together, your child is getting 100 percent of your attention.

For some families, it can be a challenge to find the right balance. Some parents go overboard and turn into helicopter parents, constantly hovering over their children. Your children need their own space. Some spouses may find themselves feeling left out when the other parent is having one-on-one kid time. Make sure each parent gets together time with each of your children. The demands of daily life may mean that at times your together time coincides with making the beds or running errands. Most parents find car rides to be excellent times to connect with their children. In my family, I suspect it's because the kids know I can't turn around and give them "the look" while driving!

Dinnertime may be one of the most overlooked opportunities to really listen to what your child has to say. Numerous studies have pointed out the benefits of family dinners. Kids who eat together four or more times a week score better on tests.[6] Family dinners are the one activity found to foster the greatest child development. One study found teens who ate an average of just over five meals a week with an adult were better adjusted, less likely to use drugs, and more motivated at school.[7]

> If you want to fight a war on drugs, sit down at your own kitchen table and talk to your own children.
> —BRIAN MCCAFFREY

Jacques Savarèse sees the benefits of family dinner every day at the New York City boys' school where he serves as guidance counselor. Or more accurately, Savarèse sees the problems with kids who don't *ever* have a meal with their parents. A guidance counselor for more than nine years, he sees a connection between children with behavior issues and a family dynamic of busy Manhattan parents who can't find time to have dinner with their child. "How about having dinner, I don't know, maybe once a week?" he asks. "How about just a family dinner on Sunday nights? Building self-respect is so important," Savarèse told me. "We love these children, but it has to come from the home."[8]

PRAISE THE POSITIVE

Which sparks a stronger reaction when you put it into your mouth— a slice of chocolate cake or a sip of milk that's gone sour? Obviously, the sour milk. While the chocolate is delicious and you would love to have more, it's that swig of rancid milk that will have you spitting and exclaiming, "Good heavens, why didn't someone throw that out!"

We tend to react the same way with regard to our children's behavior. In my house, it's a welcome surprise when my son makes his bed without a reminder. I'm pleased when the kids clear their plates and put them in the dishwasher. But truth be told, unless I make a conscious effort to remember, I rarely praise them for their good behavior. But if they lay a wet towel on my wood coffee table? Oh—you bet they'll hear about it! (Of course children need to be reminded of the rules, but don't let that be the only thing they ever hear from you as a parent.) As for making their beds and putting their dinner things away, well, they are *supposed* to do that. Why should anyone make a big deal of doing the things they're obligated to do?

Why? Because they'll do more of it if you let them know you noticed!

Psychologists know if you want to reinforce positive behavior and see it repeated, praise it. Did your child properly shake hands with someone after church and look them in the eye as you've taught them? Be sure to praise her efforts, being very specific about what your child did correctly. "Sheryl, I am so proud of the way you shook hands with the pastor. And you looked him in the eyes too! I know that made him feel so special when you said hello." Be sure your nonverbal communication is in sync with what you are saying. Smile as you offer praise, giving a little hug for emphasis. The praise should be timely (offered when the positive behavior occurs), sincere, and specific.

THE POWER OF RESPECT
If you want to reinforce positive behavior, praise it.

There's even a formula to how much praise you should give. Because "bad is stronger than good"—that is, negative emotions pack a much more powerful punch than do positive feelings[9]—experts suggest giving roughly four positive comments for every corrective (negative) comment you might make. With the groundwork done by all those positives, your child will be receptive to what you have to say. While he won't be happy hearing a reprimand, he will hear it. If he got his clothes to the hamper but didn't make the bed, first applaud him for the task well done before suggesting he at least pull up the comforter to make the bed look presentable.

For a teenager, it might be praise for giving you a heads-up to a school function. "Thanks so much for letting me know about your play-off game. I was supposed to be out of town, but since you let me know so early, I can move my trip so I won't miss your big game." Instead of complaining that your daughter's friends left a huge mess in the TV room, first say, "I love having your friends here. It's fun to hear how excited you are talking about what's happening at school," before saying, "Do you think you could get the girls to help clean up the stuff you left in the other room? It's not fair for you to have to do it by yourself later." It's a clever way of letting your darling daughter know that you are not going to be her and her friends' cleaning service!

Believe it or not, some ways of praising are better than others. You could praise someone by comparing her to others, pointing out that she did something better, faster, or more accurately than someone else. Who doesn't like knowing they were among the best at something? Another option might be to applaud someone's grasp of a situation, how well he mastered a task or how well he seems to understand something. Then there are the offhanded "good job" and "nice work" comments that often get tossed around.

A group of researchers from Reed College in Oregon wanted to see if one form of praise was more effective than another.[10] Would students be more motivated on upcoming challenges if they were praised for doing better than the rest (social comparison praise) or for specific skills and competencies they exhibited during a challenge (mastery praise)? After having a group of fourth- and fifth-grade students work on a series of puzzles during controlled experiments, one group of kids was given positive feedback comparing them to the other students, such as "Nice work! You're better at this than most kids!" and "Most kids don't do as well as that!" Another group of children did the experiments and received feedback pertaining to their own effort. "Nice work! You're becoming an expert at this. You've learned how to solve these." The kids then filled out a questionnaire measuring what kinds of things motivated them ("I read because I am interested" and "I like hard work") before choosing one of two other tasks, another puzzle situation and a drawing task.

The children who were praised for their efforts and skill (mastery praise) were more intrinsically motivated—that is, they were more likely to do a task for the sheer enjoyment of the exercise. They also tended to take on harder challenges than the kids who'd been told they were better than their peers (social comparison). As the researchers explained, the mastery praise "focused children's attention on building competence rather than proving it."

In addition, the researchers found that when a child had previously received praise comparing him or her to other children, the *absence* of such praise in the future actually had a negative effect. Since not all children can always be at the top, comparison praise can be especially damaging for low-achieving children.[11]

> Praise is like sunlight to the human spirit: we cannot flower and grow without it.
> —JESS LAIR

Based on these research findings, the better way to praise your child for a great grade on a test is "Wow! I can see by this grade that you really know your algebra" as opposed to "I bet you had the best grade in the class."

Comparison praise emphasizes a moment in time in which the child emerged the victor. Implicit in that recognition is the acknowledgment that the next time, the child could fall short. Mastery praise communicates the child's accomplishments in terms of the talent he's honed and the expertise he's developed, lasting accomplishments that can be built upon and enhanced in the future.

IGNORE THE NEGATIVE

Imagine there is a green elephant sitting in the corner of the room you're in. Now try to read on and not think of that green elephant. It is virtually impossible. It's almost as hard to ignore those behaviors in which you don't want your child engaged. It's the flip side of praising the positive. Yet the NYU Child Study Center's Harold Koplewicz swears by it.

"The best way to eliminate behavior is to ignore it," Dr. Koplewicz told me. Especially those little annoyances and misbehaviors that tend to drive parents crazy. Kids who interrupt are a great example. My friend has one. It is unbelievably frustrating to try to have a chat with my friend when her little girl constantly interrupts with one question or another. I am not sure which is more frustrating: the interrupting child or the fact that her mother keeps stopping what she's saying to answer whatever her child absolutely, positively *must* know that instant. Dr. Koplewicz's prescription? "If you want a child to stop talking, tell them nicely that you can't answer their questions now and then ignore the behavior. Then ask someone else a question. They'll quickly realize you aren't going to respond."

THE POWER OF RESPECT

The best way to eliminate unwanted behavior is to ignore it.

If you set out sneakers, and your toddler insists on wearing pink rubber rain boots on a hot sunny day, her feet will be uncomfortable, not yours. If your teenager insists on listening to headbanging music that gives you a migraine, you can respect his music choice (within reason) if he respects your hearing by plugging in headphones. If your thirteen-year-old speaks rudely to you when you are riding in the car, do not answer her until she starts to speak to you the way one properly does to a parent, and then praise her for finally coming around. "I am so glad to hear you speaking properly," you might say. "It hurt my feelings when you used that rude tone with me." In this case, you have praised the good behavior, ignored the bad, and explained why the misbehavior was hurtful to you.

It's important to point out that ignoring bad behavior is *not* tacitly approving it by letting it go unnoticed. Major infractions, meltdowns, and tantrums that can lead to destruction of property or personal injury must be stopped before any harm is done. But in ignoring the negative, what you have really done is not reinforce the negative behavior by putting the spotlight on it with your comments. A review of more than forty different studies exploring the connection between reinforcing feedback and resultant behavior found that children cease negative behaviors and have more positive responses "where the relationship between a child's behavior and the consequences of that behavior is clearly detectable."[12]

DEFINE YOUR RULES

If you could wave a magic wand, what would you want your family's interaction to be like? What rules are inviolable for you? How do you wish your children would interact with you? How would you like to interact with them? This is a wonderful opportunity for your family to get together and draft a vision of what family life could be like, with each member contributing his or her own ideas. It is a potent way to put the Power of Respect to work in your home. Here's an example of how it might play out.

The Morrisons are a typical suburban family. Dad's a business executive who's concerned lately that company sales are down and the firm may soon have to start trimming staff or hours. Mom works half days at a nonprofit and hopes to go back to work full-time when the kids are older. Their son Fredrick, age fourteen, is on the school basketball and soccer teams. He is in the adolescent phase where he feels like his parents are mainly annoying and almost always embarrassing. Fredrick does, however, still remember the times when he and his dad used to go fishing. It's been a long time since their last trip.

Rachael is ten. She's addicted to the Disney Channel, spends hours talking on the phone to her three best friends, and has a dog she adores.

Finally, there is Connor. He's six years old and in first grade, where he's a bit overwhelmed by the large number of kids in his school. He adores his older brother and doesn't understand why his big sister, who used to be like a second mother to him, lately just yells at him to go away.

Mr. and Mrs. Morrison sense the cohesive family feeling that used to permeate their household has disappeared. It seems everyone is going in different directions. Mrs. Morrison would like to lasso everyone and try to bring them back together. Instead of everyone living separate lives under one roof, she'd like to see her family more aware of what the others are doing.

RECLAIM YOUR FAMILY

Start by asking each family member what he or she wishes were different about family life. Ask them to name the deal breakers—the rules that are never to be broken, such as cheating, stealing, and lying. What responsibilities are not to be shirked? Are expectations about chores clear—and reasonable? Does Mom always have to be in charge of cooking dinner? Perhaps Dad or an older child can take over a day or two. It's a great opportunity to foster a child's independence and help him understand smart nutrition. Are there limits to the amount of time your kids are allowed to spend on the computer, video games, or music player? Discuss what you believe the limits should be and solicit feedback from your children. They may point out your ideal limit for time online is unrealistic, given the amount of research they need to do for homework.

Are family dinners something that need to be given greater priority in your home? After-school activities and long work hours can sometimes eat away at dinnertime. Is breakfast an opportunity you could seize to bring the family together? Setting the alarm just fifteen minutes earlier might be all it takes to get everyone up and around the kitchen table together. Our family shares every breakfast and most dinners together. In the mornings, we mention stories in the newspaper of interest and discuss them with the kids or try to explain why a particular story is getting heavy play on the morning news shows. At night, even if my husband and I have to go out later, I make dinner and we sit together, discussing how our days went. Since kids rarely volunteer anything about what went on at school, I sometimes resort to my fail-safe conversation starter: did anyone get in trouble at school today? Chances are something out of the ordinary happened, and that question usually evokes a spirited response.

THE POWER OF RESPECT

Make family dinners a priority in your home.

As you discuss and define your family's rules, you may want to be judicious about which rules will be your deal breakers. If you have a teenage son who insists on wearing baggy pants, you might choose to let that pass on a daily basis but insist he dress in proper pants and a jacket when going out for a family dinner or to religious services. You might draw the line across the board at tattoos as absolutely forbidden in your family. The point is, it's your family. Your values. Your rules. You decide what they are. Let the children vote, but not veto. After all, you are the parent. You decide. But you demonstrate respect to your children when you let them know, in an age-appropriate way, why the rules are what they are, and listen to their feedback.

After you clearly define the rules for your family, then make sure everyone understands the consequences for violating the rules. Harold Koplewicz suggests parents be judicial in meting out punishments. He uses the analogy of the gambler to explain. "If you have a wad of money and go into a casino, you wouldn't put it all on one number the first time around. You would dole it out," he explains. "If you take the whole wad of money and punish the kid with the whole wad, it's too severe. You've got to make the punishment appropriate to the misbehavior." If a child broke something, does he pay for it by doing extra chores? Does he lose a play date? Does he lose his video, computer, or television time?

When my children were young, I used a time-out chair in the corner of the dining room as a form of discipline. Although this form of discipline works in many families, with my son it was an utter failure. I once sentenced him to three minutes in time-out and dutifully sat him in the small chair facing the corner. About a minute and a half later, I checked to see how the little imp was doing. He was still in the chair—but he had moved it to a different

> It is only through raising expectations and striving for excellence that our children can reach their full potential.
>
> —GOV. BRAD HENRY

corner of the room. I did everything I could not to let my son see me smile!

The discipline that did work with my son was a different form of time-out. Instead of putting my son in the time-out chair, I put whatever was the favored toy of the moment on top of the refrigerator. It was right there in plain sight, but I told him it would only be returned when "good behavior" merited the toy's release from "refrigerator prison." (The special toy that was the transitional item for sleeping was not eligible for refrigerator prison. I felt like that would be too distressing.)

During your family meeting to discuss your family's rules and consequences, this might also be the time when you point out what you're really doing when you ignore your kids' negative behavior. You might say, "There have been times when you have yelled at me, and it hurts my ears. I hope you don't ever yell at me again, but if you do, I'm going to ignore you until you talk in a voice that doesn't hurt me." It will probably take a few sessions of follow-through, but your children will eventually figure it out.

> Train up a child in the way he should go, and when he is old he will not depart from it.
> —PROVERBS 22:6

SPELL OUT—AND ACT OUT—RESPECT

In our home, my husband and I try to act out respectful behavior. Kids model what they see and eventually adopt those same habits. Every morning, I am generally on the computer writing. When my husband finishes his workout, he makes the coffee and then brings me my special cup with my coffee just the way I like it. I am so appreciative of that simple, considerate act. This past summer, I realized where it comes from. His parents were visiting us, and I saw my father-in-law do exactly the same thing. He fixed my mother-in-law's coffee, brought it to her at the kitchen table, and then proceeded to prepare her breakfast. My husband's morning ritual is an exact replica of what he saw his father do when he was a child.

Model for your children the behavior you want to see from them. When your spouse treats you with respect, praise him in front of the children. When the kids join us for breakfast, I often say, "Do you know how nice Daddy is? He always brings me my coffee while I'm on the computer writing. That is the best start to my day." He also fixes the children's cereal or makes their toast. I make a point to let our children know how lucky they are to have a dad like that. The kids are reminded of what a considerate dad they have, rather than falling into the trap of taking his service for granted—and my husband will likely continue his morning rituals, feeling appreciated and valued for his efforts.

For makeup artist Laura Geller, it's been more than forty years since she saw the Power of Respect in action and she hasn't forgotten it a bit. She told me, "I remember that when I was growing up, two of my closest friends were sisters, Jodi and Amy. Their dad, Murray, was always bringing home young men or women who had challenges, and who were working at just about anything to make ends meet. Sometimes he brought home the guy who collected the carriages at our local supermarket. Sometimes it would be the local hobos who stationed themselves outside my friend's dad's jewelry store."

Jodi and Amy lived across the street. Laura told me she couldn't recall a time when her neighbor wasn't doing something to try to help these people who were down on their luck. He not only made sure they had a hot meal, Laura recalled, "He even went so far as give them a place to live! There were times when his 'guests' were met with raised eyebrows by neighbors and family members. He did not think twice. He opened his home and his family to these young people."

That was more than forty years ago. Murray died a few months ago, and at his funeral were dozens of people who had not seen the family in years but never forgot what Murray had done. Tribute after tribute came, each of them sharing how their lives were unalterably changed by the bit of respect and dignity Murray had extended to them when times were tough. It was a stunning tribute to the man with the generous spirit.

"As a grown woman myself now," Laura said, "when I think back on this man who lived directly across the street from me in a small town where everyone knew what was happening in each other's lives, I realize that for my friends Jodi and Amy, and their whole family, the funeral was a long overdue gift. To have their father, husband, and grandfather honored and paid tribute to by so many people whose lives he had changed, I just wish he could have heard the tributes for himself." Then Laura added, "But somehow, I think he always knew the impact he made on these individuals. After all, he lived the experience of being generous of spirit."

THE POWER OF RESPECT
Model for your children the behavior you want from them.

Let your kids know the kind of respectful behavior you hope to see from them. Model respect for your kids. Talk with them about the ways a child can show respect. Celebrate them when they get it right. Teach them the Golden Rule. Show them how a proper handshake feels. Let them know it's respectful to let others share their opinions first. It's respectful to be on time and not keep people waiting. It is respectful to pick up a piece of litter in the hall, even if you didn't drop it. It's respectful to put your dishes in the dishwasher after a meal. Maybe your child forgot. Instead of nagging, you might tell your daughter, "I saw you forgot to clear your plate tonight. I already put it in for you, but can you come help me clear away the serving bowls?" Her error is corrected respectfully, and clear instructions on how she is supposed to behave are handed out. She'll probably get it right next time.

Respect Tips for Parents

- Practice the Golden Rule.
- Be polite—shake hands correctly, stand for adults, let ladies go first.
- Be prompt.
- Keep unkind comments to yourself.
- Let others go first in lines and in conversation.
- Be true to your word—show up when you said you would and keep your promises.

It takes time on your part to raise a respectful kid. Several years ago, I complimented an Austrian friend on how incredibly mannerly her two sons were. They elegantly bent and shook my hand in the exquisite way European men do. They were just boys, ages thirteen and fifteen, but they had the gallant air of someone much older. Their mother, Suzanne, laughed and said, "You have no idea how much we worked at this. I would pretend to be their 'dear Aunt Agnes' coming for a visit. They would greet me at the door, usher me to a chair, and offer me a cup of tea." Suzanne said that if the boys made a misstep, "Aunt Agnes" turned into a shrew and whacked them with her handbag, which meant they had to start from scratch. "We made a game of it," she told me, "and they loved when I pretended to be upset." Eventually, her sons became adept at the social graces. I have no doubt that as those boys go out on their own, young ladies will swoon over their spectacular manners.

Parents can play a much bigger role than they think in helping kids avoid risky behaviors. A 2006 study done for SADD (Students Against Destructive Decisions) found that teens whose parents set specific expectations with clear consequences are less likely to have driven while under the influence of alcohol or drugs, more likely to drive within the speed limit, and more likely stick to rules about driving at night or with multiple passengers in the car.[13]

THE POWER OF RESPECT
Parents can have great influence on their kids' behavior.

Parents can help guide their children in making their own choices about what their value system will be. Adolescence is a time when children push away from their parents. But while the physical parental presence may be reduced, a parent's influence on a teen's values doesn't have to be.

Talk with your children about how they will handle upcoming challenges. Help them to articulate what they believe. Resist the urge to impose your values on your child, but do explain why you believe as you do. Your child may not want to discuss his or her answers with you. But these questions can get the thought process started and give your teenagers an opportunity to consider the options before they find themselves on the hot seat. If your children feel good about themselves and have learned the Power of Respect at home, chances are

> Research shows that parents are the single biggest influence on children—if you are worried about your teen and drugs, talk to them.
> —JOHN WALTERS

the value system they devise for themselves will be one you both can embrace. So what should be among the areas you discuss?

- *Dating and intimacy.* Statistically, there is great pressure on teens to be sexually active. How will you handle it? Do you know the facts? Do you really know all the ways STDs can be transmitted?
- *Friendships.* What does it take to be a good friend? How will you speak up for yourself? What's the difference between being a pal and being a doormat? What's your view on "friends with benefits"? And if you don't know what that means, you need to get more familiar with teen life right now!
- *Assertiveness.* What are your goals? How will you assert yourself to achieve them? What do you consider your "rights"? How will you protect them?
- *Role models.* Are there kids in your circle you admire? Adults you'd like to emulate? How do you define *respect*?

> Attention to the virtues is one of the important ties that bind a family together.
> —WILLIAM BENNETT

That last question may be the most important. To define what respect means to them, children must take time to consider what is important to them. They experience the ego boost that comes from being recognized. They feel the confidence that comes from being trusted to make decisions. Choosing between the red shirt or the white one when you are five years old helps lay the foundation for more challenging choices later on. They analyze the hurt that comes from being ignored. The more you can help your child connect to his own feelings about what respect means and feels like, the easier it is for him to practice it.

You may be surprised at what facilitating this conversation might do for your relationship. The fact that *you,* the parent, are asking *them,* the children, what they think about respect completely changes the dynamic. Far from diminishing the parental role as authority figure, it enhances it, underscoring it with a benevolence that is both disarming and appreciated. *Dad cares what I think?* your child will probably say to himself, with a hint of disbelief. Coupled with respectful acts on your part, the message will slowly get through, no matter what age the child. Whether a youngster still at home, a teen pushing to break free of family bonds, or an adult child who may have become estranged—the Power of Respect can bring children and parents closer.

Respect Reminders

- ☐ Reinforce positive behavior with praise.
- ☐ Praise efforts without comparing to others.
- ☐ Talk about what makes one feel respected.
- ☐ Model the behavior you want to see.

3

The Glue That Keeps
Us Together

The Power of Respect in Relationships

You never know what might be waiting around the corner. Tomorrow could be just another day, notable only for the sameness of the days before. Or it could bring a surprise that takes you down a path you could have neither contemplated nor prepared for.

January 28, 2006, was that day for Lee. A suburban mother of four, she had brought her children to Florida for a Disney World vacation while their dad was out of town on a business trip. If that morning seemed special to the kids, it was only because that day they were going to ride their favorite rides at the park.

Lee is a woman who seems to handle the twists and turns of life better than most of us. She would never agree with this, but she appears to somehow float blissfully, juggling the needs of her children alongside the often unpredictable schedule her husband's job requires. Whether it's scheduling dental appointments and arranging college visits or joining her husband for a work-related evening event, Lee seems to get it all done and never seems frazzled. The Power of Respect seems evident in so many areas of her life.

"Understanding respect allows us all to move through the world with grace, to operate with the knowledge that there are things bigger than us," Lee told me. "There are moments of grace that allow us to feel the presence of everyday little miracles. But to be open to those, to really participate, is to be able to appreciate, respect, and love those who mean something in our lives." That's Lee talking on just a plain old Saturday morning. It's easy to see why she is so admired by all of her friends. It's that mind-set that enabled Lee to handle with grace the unthinkable challenge that came her way.

They didn't know it, but that day when Lee and her kids were heading off to the Magic Kingdom, halfway around the planet, their world was changing. Their dad was in Iraq in an armored vehicle, riding with the Iraqi army. The vehicle hit an IED. The land mine exploded, shattering the tank and half of their dad's head. The injury was massive, shrapnel embedded in his brain. Medics weren't sure Bob would survive.

Lee is Lee Woodruff, the wife of ABC newsman Bob Woodruff. The impact of the bomb struck the left side of Woodruff's face. Countless bits of rock and metal fragments laced his face, part of his jaw was sheared off by a rock, and another ripped his cheek. Bob's skull sustained the worst of the explosion. His skull was crushed against the left side of his head into his brain, displacing his left eye in its socket. There were massive amounts of blood. Once ABC News learned of the accident, they tracked down Lee Woodruff at Disney World. Within hours, she was on a private jet headed to Europe, not sure what awaited her when she arrived.

Lee and Bob Woodruff write movingly of their journey in their gripping best-selling book, *In an Instant.*[1] Now, nearly four years later, the physical signs of Bob's trauma are virtually gone. The Woodruffs have used their experience to become advocates for wounded soldiers, especially those with traumatic brain injuries, which roughly one in every five returning servicemen and women wounded in Iraq and Afghanistan have sustained. Though most in the television world are noted for their self-absorbed ways, the Woodruffs have used their notoriety to create the Bob Woodruff Foundation to raise money to make sure every wounded soldier receives the same state-of-the-art treatment and care that helped Bob recover.[2]

Lee and Bob met in college and got married in 1988. She told me that from the moment she met Bob, she "respected his brain, his energy and curiosity, his background, and his ethics and morality." Her love grew from that. "If you don't respect someone, can you love them?" Lee asks. Answering her own question, she replied, "I'd contest that isn't love. It's probably lust."

THE POWER OF RESPECT
The Power of Respect brings fairness to marriage.

In any marriage, there are disagreements—and the Woodruffs are certainly typical in that regard. Yet Lee Woodruff contends respect for one another has allowed them to fight fair. She told me, "It allows you to keep your dignity intact. You can put the other fellow first when that's appropriate. Respect in a marriage means factoring that person into the equation and putting someone else's needs on an equal footing with yours." She calls that "one of life's gifts."

> Respect and love are the two cornerstones in a marriage on which everything else is built.
> —LEE WOODRUFF

Foundation for a Strong Marriage

If love and respect are the foundation stones for a strong marriage, it's no surprise Jim and Ina Hopkins are still going strong. After thirty-two years of marriage, this is how Jim introduces his wife, Ina: "I have the privilege of being married to this wonderful woman." It's the way Jim has been introducing Ina for as long as she can remember and she loves it. She says, "My smile extends from ear to ear to know that my husband not only feels that way about me but also would share that sentiment in public. My heart fills with love for him each time."

It's now more than three decades since the college sweethearts were married. She was a brilliant graduate with a public relations degree. He was a go-getter who'd majored in business. Ina had no idea how much "going" she'd be getting to do. From Georgia to Illinois to Pennsylvania and stops in between, the couple frequently pulled up stakes and moved to the next town. Friends learned to record their address in pencil because they knew it would soon change.

Ina reflects back on those days. "We lived the corporate lifestyle," she recalled, "moving too frequently to set down roots. While we have dear friends scattered around the country, it always felt like we were 'outside looking in.'" She told me a friend of hers is a Navy wife who told her, "I know how to move; I don't know how to stay." Ina Hopkins could relate. She said, "Moving becomes a way of life."

There was a period in the Hopkinses' marriage when Jim was living out of a travel kit, whether at home or in one of the countless international countries he visited. Why bother unpacking your toiletries when you know you'll soon be on another plane? Ina shouldered the burden of home life, which at times was heavy. "When he was home, he was too weary to notice that the bills were paid, grass cut, and our daughter had all her shots," she told me, looking back. "I merely wanted some respect and verbal acknowledgment for keeping things rolling." But Ina was sensitive enough to recognize that Jim needed some appreciation too. She said, "He needed my respect for the work he was doing and the pressure he was under. Thank goodness we worked through those years."

I knew when I called Ina Hopkins to ask her about the role the Power of Respect can play in a marriage that she would have some pearls of wisdom. She is one of my dearest friends from college, the sorority sister I wanted to be just like. I couldn't have picked a better source.

In America, 2.2 million couples marry every year, and half of them will end up divorced.[3] Ina says the reason shouldn't be a secret to anyone. Neglect. It's human nature, she says, to discount those closest to us. Ina says, "It's important to not only love your partner but give them true respect and show them that you adore them."

Tips for a Respectful Marriage

- Acknowledge what makes your partner special. Praise everyday chores he or she does for your benefit.
- Brag about your partner in front of others *and* your partner.
- Tell your partner she (or he) is beautiful (or handsome).
- Don't promise what you can't deliver.
- Share the load, and share your day.
- Listen to and respect your partner's view.

Ina recommends you try to recognize all the ways your partner is special. Of her husband, Jim, she says, "He is the handiest man I know and, more times than not, completely willing to tackle a project on the 'honey-do' list when asked. He is also the best son, nephew, husband, and father I know." Ina is vocal in praising her husband's wisdom and often prefaces a reference to him as "My sweet Jim."

No doubt about it, a lot of the everyday aspects of life are just plain boring. Life gets very busy, very crazy, and very stressful. Making sure the kids have socks, getting the furnace serviced, cleaning the gutters—someone has to do it. Unless you live alone, someone has done something for you. If there is food in the cupboard and you haven't been to the grocery store, someone else has. Thank them for making the trip. Standing in those lines isn't fun—they did you a favor by keeping you away from the grocer's. Ina says, "Taking the time and making the time to notice and acknowledge that your clothes are back from the cleaners, that your favorite juice is in the refrigerator, and the drip irrigation was altered to water the new plants is critical to maintaining a healthy marriage."

"Thank you" consists of just eight letters that form two of the most meaningful words in the English vocabulary. Rather than looking at these necessary chores as a burden, Ina sees them as a way to show her love and respect for her husband. "Those are the ways you show respect to your partner, knowing that it will make their day a little brighter," she told me.

> The spaces between your fingers were created so that another's could fill them in.
> —UNKNOWN

What do you admire about your partner? Have you told him or her? When I met my Swedish-born husband, I was astonished by the breadth of his knowledge. Whether it was opera and art, or world politics and the economy, he just knew so much *more* than I did. When we played Trivial Pursuit, he got all the culture questions right. I excelled only at sports and naming television shows. Twenty years later, I am still astonished at what he knows and am still trying to figure out when he's learning all these things. Karl knows I marvel at his intellect, but I probably don't tell him often enough. It's a common oversight.

After all her years of marriage, Ina still loves to hear her husband's compliments, especially when they are given in front of a new acquaintance. She says it always takes men by surprise, and she believes it makes other husbands think twice about how often they compliment their wives.

We all like to hear we look good. The longer a relationship lasts, the less either partner looks like the fresh-faced person in the engagement photos. Men and women both need to hear they look attractive. An unexpected flower or a heartfelt note under the pillow is a small gesture that is returned multifold. The most precious gifts I have received from my husband and children are not the ones that have come in boxes, but the ones found in envelopes. Those sincere, love-filled letters are my real treasures. They lift my spirits every time I reread them.

For Lee and Bob Woodruff, the year 2006 required tenacity. The severity of Bob's injuries and challenge of recuperation were enough of a strain. Add to that the burden of the public spotlight the family was in. As the newly named anchor of ABC's premiere newscast, *World News Tonight,* Bob had one of the most visible jobs in television. His

> A wedding anniversary is the celebration of love, trust, partnership, tolerance, and tenacity. The order varies for any given year.
> —PAUL SWEENEY

battle to recover was being followed by both legitimate and tabloid papers as well as human interest television programs. Reporters were scrambling for an "exclusive" story on Bob's recovery. Those cornerstones of marriage, respect and love, were lifesavers during the challenging time.

"When Bob was injured, respect was the one thing I needed to give him above anything else during his recovery," Lee recalled. "He was missing words and names. His cognitive function was scrambled." Above all, the caring wife felt she needed to protect her husband's dignity. Only those people she could trust to respect him were allowed into Bob's life during those first weeks and months he was back home. "I shrunk our world down into a tiny pinprick of only close friends and family. I was wary of anyone I didn't know I could fully trust might blab to colleagues that he couldn't say *Iraq* but could pronounce *Mahmoud Ahmadinejad* [the president of Iran]. I watched over him like a mother lion."

Lee may have protected her injured husband like a lioness, but she continued to respect him like the adoring wife she had always been. "I never let anything in my manner show him that I respected him any less or loved him any differently. When he couldn't think of simple words, I treated him with the same respect I had accorded him when he could speak three languages and read five papers and memorize whole pages of text." Though she confesses she privately feared the what-ifs: *What if Bob didn't fully recover? How would she love him? How would she respect him?* She kept those fears deeply hidden.

Today Bob and Lee are moving forward in their lives. Their foundation is doing important work for families experiencing the kind of crisis they survived. Their eldest son has followed in their footsteps to their alma mater. Lee is now sharing her profound wisdom with a wider circle through her best-selling books and lectures. Bob has resumed his reporting career for ABC News. It's unlikely that any medical expert would argue that Lee Woodruff's Power of Respect and depth of love for her husband were not critically important to his spectacular recovery. They are an inspiring testament to the Power of Respect.

THE POWER OF RESPECT
The Power of Respect helps couples weather challenges.

A MARRIAGE BUILT ON RESPECT

Fifty-four years is a long time, and that's exactly how long Joan and Sandy Weill have been married. They met when they were in college, and in the early days of married life, he earned so little as a ground-level runner at a brokerage house that they couldn't have survived without her salary as an elementary school teacher. Today Weill is one of the wealthiest men in America, having built the financial giant Citigroup, which last year received billions of federal money after it collapsed under its own weight. The roller coaster of lean times, extraordinary wealth, and life in the public eye could be expected to take a toll on any couple, but the Weills say they've lasted because they have emphasized being partners.

Lasting, respect-filled marriages usually do function as a partnership. "I think the best rule is to not try and force your way, but try and understand where the other person is coming from," says the former Citigroup chairman and CEO. You might think Sandy Weill is talking about his strategy of using acquisitions for transforming a small low-end lender into one of the largest financial institutions in the world. He's not. He's talking about marriage, something he could also qualify as expert at given his fifty-four-year marriage to his wife, Joan. We spoke just a couple of weeks before their wedding anniversary.

Over their five-plus decades of marriage, Weill said he's come to believe that differences between a husband and wife can be useful. "I think to marry someone who is a mirror image of yourself would be very difficult. I think you're better off having a relationship with someone who comes at issues differently than you do. That creates much more of a balance."

Weill gives his life partner a lot of credit for his success. He told me, "Joan has had an amazing influence on me. I was pretty shy when I met her, and she helped my sense of humor come out. She helped me to not think so much about me and instead listen to what the other person is saying and be responsive to their feelings." Weill said it was his wife's prodding that helped him appreciate that scheduling work-related events on weekends was not respecting employees' family responsibilities. For her part, Joan Weill has said she appreciated participating in his career and his sharing what was going on with the business. "It was helpful to our relationship," she said.

Even after a half century of marriage, though, Weill is the first to say marriage takes work. "Marriage and love are evolving things that are built on respect," he said. "If people would spend only a fraction of the energy that they spend on business on trying to get ahead in their relationships with their spouses, they would be much better off and have a real partnership."

It's amazing how many couples are clueless about what their spouses are doing when they are apart. What are your spouse's challenges at work, whether that work is at a job or a home? The Weills are adamant that their marriage has lasted because Joan was kept in the loop about Sandy's business life. Whether as a sounding board, adviser, or just to have someone to listen to, let your spouse know what's going on in your work life and during your time apart. In a non-annoying way, ask about what they are doing. It is a way of showing respect.

You may divvy up household duties between you, but each

should be kept abreast of what's going on. Imagine the shock of suddenly losing your spouse and then realizing you know absolutely nothing about the finances of your household. It's easy to see how the grief could turn to hurt. *Was I not smart enough to be entrusted with the financial information? Was I not trusted?*

Last spring, Pennsylvania mom Bonnie Sweeten disappeared after she mysteriously made a false 911 call that she and her nine-year-old daughter had been kidnapped. She was found a few days later at Disney World. Along with questions about her bizarre action, there were concerns about substantial funds missing from the charitable institution where she worked. As Mrs. Sweeten was being extradited back to her home state to face criminal charges, her husband was on television explaining he knew nothing about the family finances.[4] He said for all he knew, he might be behind on his mortgage. That is not a partnership. Even if one spouse handles the money, it's important to share the load. Each of you needs to understand how it's being spent and invested.

> Listening is a high art of loving. Ask yourself, *When was the last time I really listened to my child? My parent? My brother or sister?* When someone is ready to share, three magic words amplify your connection, and they are: "Tell me more."
>
> —REV. MARY MANIN MORRISSEY

Listening is not only a high art. It is also a key component in whether a marriage survives or collapses, as well as one of the most important tools in channeling the Power of Respect.

THE VALUE OF LISTENING

Michele Weiner-Davis began her marriage convinced she was going to do everything right. A child of divorce, Michele was sixteen when her parents split up after twenty-three years of marriage. It was a shattering experience for Michele. "I was thinking I had the East Coast version of *The Waltons*," she says. "My parents never fought. After twenty-three years, my mom said she was very unhappy and she got a divorce." Michele never saw it coming.

When Michele married her husband, she was determined to make her marriage last. In the early days of her marriage, she would greet her husband, Jim, at the door, asking how his day went, what was new, and so on. She was really trying to tune in to his day and let him know that she cared about what he did during the hours they were apart. Weiner-Davis says she emulated what her own mother did when she was girl.

"My mom was very tuned in to me," she explained. "When I came home from school, she could tell in an instant: 'How was your day? Did something go wrong? Did you have a fight at school?' She respected me and tuned in to me as a person. I took this end-of-the-day routine into my early years with my husband."

It was, as Weiner-Davis put it, "a gift returned unopened." She explained, "Jim is one of the most independent men. I would see that detached look. My 'tuning in' was not a gift to him, but an annoyance." Weiner-Davis's husband needed time on his own to decompress at the end of the day, and it was a while before his wife figured that out. "It took me years to stop talking and give him space. Not checking in when he arrived home was an unnatural act for me."

An unnatural act, but also an eye-opener. "It's not until something feels unnatural that you really know you are giving a real gift. It has to come with a little bit of discomfort because you are outside your comfort zone," Weiner-Davis relates. This revelation has been invaluable to Michele Weiner-Davis in her work.

RESPECT IS DISCOVERING
HOW YOUR PARTNER DEFINES RESPECT

Michele Weiner-Davis is a marriage counselor who calls her work with troubled couples "divorce busting."[5] In her more than twenty years of counseling work, Weiner-Davis continues to be amazed by how out of sync so many couples are. Even when they try to get the Power of Respect right, they get it wrong. "It is mind-boggling how one person's definition of respect can be so different from his or her spouse's," she exclaims. "A wife might say, 'If you respected me, you would know it is important to spend a lot of time together.' But she may be married to someone who says, 'If you respected me, you would know I need my alone time. That is how I regenerate.' One might ask, 'How can they stay together or heal when there is a problem?'

"It's a mistake that couples make, both young and old. There are two definitions of respect," Weiner-Davis says emphatically. "What makes me feel respected is not always what makes you feel respected. I tell couples that real giving is when you give your partner what he wants, whether you understand or not, whether you like it or not, whether you agree or not. That is completely irrelevant."

The first step to bringing the Power of Respect to a marriage that needs it is conversation. Weiner-Davis recommends couples sit down and discuss their wish list for the relationship. In her experience, often when couples think they're communicating, they are actually talking around each other. Here are snippets of discussions she says *don't* work:

- If you respected me, you would speak differently when you talk in front of my coworkers.

("What does that mean?" asks Weiner-Davis. "There
is too much vagueness.")

- If you respected me, you would be more understanding
of the time I need away. ("That's aiming, but not
clear enough," she says. Sometimes a spouse will try
to be accommodating but miss the mark. Weiner-Davis
says the spouse ends up feeling put upon because
he or she attempted to show respect and is getting
no appreciation for it.)

Weiner-Davis counsels couples to use precise language in talking
about their needs. "Many couples are arguing over the generalities,"
she told me. If one spouse needs to have a little time by themselves, be
specific. "It would be really great if when I come home, you could just
give me a half an hour to chill out before I dive in," Weiner-Davis
suggests you say. Maybe you need "me time" on weekends. Weiner-
Davis recommends saying this: "On the weekend, I need just half a
day to get some things done, and then I am quite willing to take over."
As Weiner-Davis puts it, "Be very specific and action oriented in saying what you want. Say, 'I need you to take the garbage out without
being asked,' instead of, 'I want you to be more considerate,' for
example. The angels are in the details. Often, couples find they can
live with what the other person wants." But it takes conversation to
find out what the partner needs—and careful listening to understand
what they are really saying.

Why is this so important?

The Number-One Factor in Divorce

"Lack of respect." That's what Marilyn Chinitz says is the number-
one factor in divorce. "If you lack respect, you are going to cheat. If
you lack respect, you are going to lie. If you really respect someone,

you know that if you do any of those things, you destroy the relationship. You destroy that person. The last thing you want to do is
destroy that person if you really love them. Respect is critical."

Marilyn Chinitz is an expert on divorce because she is intimately
involved in cleaning up the detritus left behind when marriages collapse. Chinitz is one of New York's leading divorce attorneys, having
handled well over seven hundred divorce cases. She says successful
couples work to gain their partners' respect by taking time to help, by
valuing their partners' opinions, and by being deferential and appreciative. "These elements are the means to accomplish a respectful
relationship," she counseled. "When you are respectful, it makes you
considerate. It causes you not to cause pain to someone. When that
is gone," she told me emphatically, "the marriage is gone."

Chinitz sees spouses and partners during their worst moments,
and it's given her some insights into the dynamics of marital relationships. "You know what I find?" she asked. "The longer we know
someone, sometimes the less kind and respectful we are because we
think, *Oh, they understand.* You almost take that person for granted.
Sometimes the person you are most respectful to is the stranger you
meet for ten minutes. You go to the supermarket and pay them and
you say, 'Have a wonderful day.' They think you are the most
unbelievable person," she told me.

But at home, it's often a different story. She continued, "You
stop doing that when you live with someone for a long time, and
that's the mistake. That's the mistake you make with your kids too.
You have to work at respect. When I say work at it, it should just be
your everyday routine."

The end product of the Power of Respect in a marriage is trust.
Marilyn Chinitz usually sees a wife, husband, or partner when that
bond of trust is eroded or abruptly destroyed. But when that bond of
trust is present, she says, it is actually liberating. "It reduces the need
for a spouse to monitor someone else's behavior," she explained.

"When you trust and respect people, you don't have to know every second what they are doing or what they are thinking. It gives them a sense of privacy and you the knowledge that when they gave you their word, it was solid. There is a peace in that."

Marriage counselor Michele Weiner-Davis agrees. "Trust isn't the icing on the cake," she says. "It *is* the cake. If you don't have trust in your marriage, you don't have a platform for anything." Most of the couples who come to Weiner-Davis seek her intervention in their marriage after a breach of trust, often a huge breach of trust. "I focus on helping people rebuild trust and in doing so, respect is built." She told me for couples willing to work hard, the prognosis is good. "Infidelity is not for sissies. It takes a lot of work to get a marriage back on track. If people are willing to do the hard work to rebuild the relationship and go the extra mile," she told me, "not only do they feel more connected and safe in the relationship, but it also breeds a sense of respect."

Marilyn Chinitz has seen it happen time and again—even after divorce lawyers have been called. When those nuts-and-bolts meetings begin, with attorneys trying to hash out how to permanently split a family and its assets, many times one spouse or the other realizes he or she has made a terrible mistake, even if the spouse who initiated the divorce wasn't the one who was unfaithful.

"In one particular case, my client was devastated by her husband's infidelity," she recalled. "She was such a strong, powerful, spiritual woman and it took great strength on her part to separate herself from the pain and have enough respect for her and her children to say, 'You know what? I cannot destroy all of these lives, and neither can he.'" Chinitz says the husband came to the realization that he had committed a terrible wrong, not just to his wife but to his children as well. He was devastated that his indiscretion impacted the family, and he worked hard to regain his wife's trust.

"Respect is solid stuff," Chinitz marveled. "Love kind of comes and goes. It's fickle. But respect stays there. It's the anchor. He felt enough respect and love for his children and for their mother, knowing that his children needed the security of having both parents in their daily lives, that he begged her to take him back. And she did." Chinitz describes the couple today as a solid unit, with strength of character and fortitude. Their marriage survived, happily.

RESPECT SPEAKS EVERY LANGUAGE

It was the end of the week, and Eugenia Harvey was looking forward to a long weekend away from the heat and grime of Cairo, Egypt. The American television producer had been in the Middle East working on a documentary, and it didn't look like she'd be coming home anytime soon. An escape to Bahrain would be a welcome respite.

In front of her in line was a family: a husband, his pregnant wife, and their wiggly, chubby baby. From what Ms. Harvey could make out of the conversation with the ticket agent, the husband had made some kind of mistake with their passports or tickets. For nearly an hour, he held an animated argument with the clerk, the managers, and their supervisors. Finally the family was told to step aside, and the line behind them slowly inched forward.

It was beastly hot, and the mother with the squirmy baby was fully veiled in the black

> If you go looking for a friend, you're going to find they're very scarce. If you go out to be a friend, you'll find them everywhere.
> —ZIG ZIGLAR

abaya and *niqab.* Only her eyes were visible. They were teary and filled with humiliation. As Ms. Harvey told me, "She was sweating bullets, trying to calm the baby and fighting back tears. She dared not disrespect her husband."

The American reached into her handbag and pulled out a package of tissues and handed them to the veiled mother. "A look of gratitude replaced the humiliation she had shown just moments earlier," Ms. Harvey related. "She muttered *shokran* [thank you]. I nodded back and gave her a universal gesture of 'Girl, I understand,' and moved along."

They were two women whose cultures could not have been more different. Yet the shared experience of the travails of travel and the common female bond of caring brought them together for a brief instant. The Power of Respect speaks in all languages.

RESPECT MEANS REACHING OUT

The Whistle Stop café was jammed that night, with waitresses hustling back and forth taking orders and picking up steaming hot plates at the kitchen window. Back in the kitchen, the cooks' hands were a blur as they prepared meal after meal. The parking lot outside was filled, and there was a kind of electricity in the air.

It was an unusual kind of excitement because lately in Birmingham, Michigan, there hadn't been much to get excited about. One of Detroit's northwest suburbs, the town has borne the brunt of the collapse of the automobile industry. Unemployment here is above the national average. Even the local school system had to lay off staff members. All that made the hubbub at the Whistle Stop all the more noteworthy.

On this evening, and every evening for the entire week, the patrons here could order off the menu, but they didn't have to pay the price listed. For one week, Whistle Stop owner Matt Rafferty was letting patrons pay what they could. It was one man's way of letting his neighbors know times may be tough, but they're not alone.

"It just seemed like the right thing to do," Rafferty says. "I saw all this negativity on the news and I thought, *I know I am not Superman, I know I am not going to change the economy, but what can I do to get people out of the house again and give people a reason to smile?* You know, some people hadn't been out to eat for a year because they can't afford it. I thought, *Hey, I have a restaurant. If I were in that position, if I could give what I could afford to pay for a meal—that would get me out of the house.* The idea grew from there."

To put it mildly, pretty much everyone around Matt Rafferty thought he'd lost his mind. The thirty-five-year-old restaurant owner is not a wealthy man. He's a divorced father of two, trying to raise his kids and run the diner he bought five years ago. Birmingham is where he grew up. He came back home a few years ago, gave up a suit-and-tie job, and returned to his first love, cooking. When he was a little boy, Rafferty used to eat at the Whistle Stop with his family.

Like most other businesses in his hometown, Rafferty's restaurant was suffering the effects of the economy too. His own business was down about 30 percent. To try to cut costs, he's been waiting tables, taking over a shift cooking, even doing the heavy cleaning when the diner closes for the night. The last thing he could afford was to give away dinners for a week. Still, he says, it just seemed like the right thing to do. "I believe, in general," he says, "if you do the right thing it just comes back to you."

For one week, the Whistle Stop had a line out the door, people waiting for their own pay-what-you-can meal, many of them exactly the kinds of families he was hoping he'd get to serve. There was the unemployed single mother of four whose children have to share a room. They barely have enough money for groceries, much less enough to go out. There was the family with two autistic boys. Both parents had lost their jobs, and their first priority was to buy medication for their boys. They hadn't been out to eat in two years. Rafferty says one of the boys gave him a hug, and the parents later sent him a heartfelt letter.

"I had so many people come in and seek me out. They were crying real tears and hugging me like I just saved their life or donated my kidney to them or something. I mean, all I was doing was giving them a meal." Weeks after the promotion, Rafferty is still incredulous about it all. "They were bawling and saying that God is going to bless me. These people, they were real. They didn't come in scripted. The emotion was real."

Everyone who worked at the Whistle Stop pitched in. The waitresses gave up their salaries and worked just for tips. The cooks volunteered to take a reduced wage. Of course, human nature being what it is, there were indeed people who took advantage of the Whistle Stop's hospitality, ones who drove up in a BMW and then left five dollars for their meal. Rafferty encouraged his staff to look beyond those kinds of people. "I said if someone gives you less money than you deserve, then you smile and you thank them and ask them to come back," he related. "It's not easy, but they will be miserable later, and you will be fine with yourself."

In fact, it's been more than fine. The publicity surrounding the promotion has put the Whistle Stop back on the map. Business is still not what it was, but it's back up. Rafferty has been getting letters of praise from around the country, some of which have twenty-dollar bills tucked inside as a pay-it-forward gesture. The restaurateur has even heard from a production company about making his idea into a television show! It *is* pretty exciting stuff, but Matt Rafferty is focusing on a different thrill. He saw the Power of Respect at work.

"I am a divorced single man. I know when times are tough, one of the first things that goes is the family relationship. It's really easy to start pointing fingers and take frustrations out on each other. What did I see that week? Respect. When they were sitting in my booth, these families were smiling and laughing. All the hardship of the last few years seemed to disappear. That was worth its weight right there."

Matt Rafferty knows he gave his customers that week something much more sustaining than a tasty meal. Who knows if luck will change for any of them, but that night, he gave them a lifeline, a tangible sign that there are bright spots in the world, there are people who are good, and not every day will be dark. He gave them respect. Each of his customers was served with dignity and a smile. There were no paupers those nights at the Whistle Stop . . . just a diner filled with princes.

> A man who has friends must himself be friendly.
> —PROVERBS 18:24

CONNECTING WITH OTHERS

If respect is the grease that helps society move smoothly, relationships are the glue that holds it together. Whether it's sharing tissues with a distraught stranger or an affordable meal with neighbors down on their luck, the Power of Respect makes you want to connect with others. The Power of Respect fosters compassion and altruism. Researchers debate whether the motivation is egotistic (it makes me feel good to help others) or empathetic.[6] Either way, a good deed has been done. It may also be that these respectful acts bring people closer to one another.

Friendship is an often overlooked source of strength for individuals. The support of friends is often more important than that of family members because friendship is optional.[7] Family is stuck with you. You were chosen by your friends. Women tend to have more intimate friendships, with confidants often coming from shared interests.[8] Men, on the other hand, may have buddies whom they rely on for

> In poverty and other
> misfortunes of life,
> true friends are a
> sure refuge.
>
> —ARISTOTLE

activities such as a weekend round of golf or pickup basketball game, but they usually look to their spouses as the persons in whom they confide.[9] In fact, married people say friendship is five times more important in a marriage than physical intimacy.

THE NEED TO BELONG

The need to belong, to connect with other people, is one of man's most basic motivations. We gather in groups and form relationships for protection, for social interaction, for procreation. When we receive messages from the world around us that tell us we are included, that we matter, that our presence or our opinions are valued, we are elevated. Our moods lift; our spirits lighten. If we are valued, our thinking goes, then it follows there must be something about us that is worthy.

THE POWER OF RESPECT
The Power of Respect helps people feel like they belong.

How this impacts people varies greatly. The more important it is to a person to belong, the more significant the Power of Respect is. People who are desperately concerned about others' opinions of them will be much more sensitive to perceived or real slights. One study looking into this phenomenon concluded, "If people are especially concerned about their reputations, they respond significantly . . . to variations in respect. In contrast, when people do not care as much about their reputations, variations in respect . . . do not influence people's reactions."[10]

Because it's impossible to know who has a psychological need to belong and who doesn't, it simply makes sense to treat everyone with respect. People who feel respected experience positive emotions, making them more creative, happier, and more helpful. It works, whether you're being respectful to your spouse or the man at the shoeshine stand.

THE POWER OF RESPECT AT WORK

The Power of Respect makes relationships at work better too. In fact, having a friend at work makes employees better workers. Workers who say there is no one they are particularly friendly with at work have only an 8 percent chance of being engaged in their job. Employees who do have friendships on the job are happier. Forty-three percent of them say they've been praised within a week, 37 percent say they get encouragement on the job, 28 percent say someone has talked with them about advancing in the organization, and 27 percent say they feel their job is important and that their opinions count.[11] As you'll see in chapter 5, that is a key barometer for a happy, stable workforce.

Workplace friendships also invoke the Power of Respect, because when people have personal connections, they act in a respectful way that translates to greater productivity. A study done by Karen Jehn of the University of Pennsylvania's Wharton School found that when friends work side-by-side, they do socialize more, but the friendship actually acts like grease facilitating communication, which can improve job performance.[12]

The study assembled two groups of teams together and asked them to follow very strict instructions in building Tinkertoy sets. Teams in one group knew each other, but only superficially, while teams in the other group were very close friends. The good friends had a 62 percent success rate in building the projects correctly. The acquaintances got less than half of them correct (48.8 percent). Jehn believes the comfort level between the good friends made it possible for ideas to be challenged constructively because they felt safe with each other. The teams that knew each other only slightly were observed to be almost too polite. They tended not to criticize for fear of offending someone. Based on this research, employers might enjoy greater productivity if they were to host occasional mixers, pizza parties, or picnics to encourage more collegiality among staff. You will see more about how the Power of Respect can make a difference at work in chapter 5.

The Destructive Power of Disrespect

You can't talk about the Power of Respect without examining the consequences of what happens when respect is absent. The Power of Disrespect is hugely destructive.

Respect is a door that swings both ways. When customers don't feel they are respected, they take their business elsewhere. Medical patients say they value doctors' interpersonal skills *more* than their medical training or knowledge of the latest treatments. A recent survey found 85 percent of U.S. adults say it is extremely important for their doctor to be respectful. Eighty-four percent say they want a doctor who listens carefully and is easy to talk to. The survey found that people will switch doctors when they don't feel their physicians listen to them carefully. Feeling rushed during appointments is a common patient complaint, but now patients are doing something about it. Fourteen percent of patients switched doctors because they felt their physician didn't listen carefully. Twelve percent said the doctor didn't spend enough time with them, and 11 percent felt they weren't treated with respect.[13] As America debates how to restructure its health-care system, leaders would be well advised to consider the role respect plays in the healing process.

Friendships are like flowers— they grow best when they are nurtured. The best fertilizer for friendships is time, and without time together, friendships wither.

Anne thought she had a good friendship with Lisa, a public relations executive. Not only had

> Nothing valuable can be lost by taking time.
>
> —ABRAHAM LINCOLN

they worked on a few projects together, but over the years they had traded career advice and had lots of enjoyable lunches or the occasional drink after work. But lately, every time they set up a date for breakfast or lunch, Lisa inevitably cancels it. Worse, to Anne, Lisa has her assistant make the call.

As Anne sees it, she's an "expendable friend" to Lisa. She feels like Lisa considers her someone to spend time with when there's nothing better to do. She knows Lisa has a challenging career, but so does Anne. The often-canceled lunches have left Anne feeling disrespected. Recently, Lisa canceled another get-together, the third in a row. Anne has decided to move her fair-weather friend to one of her less important circles of acquaintances.

The disrespect Anne felt from her friend's unreliability pales in comparison to what's happening with teens. Disregard for self and others is growing. Remember the headlines, mentioned in chapter 1? Victoria Lindsay thought she was going to her friend's house for a sleepover when one girl suddenly started taunting, then attacking her. Eight girls, many of them high school cheerleaders, were part of an attack that was videotaped so it could later be put online. Victoria was left with a concussion and hearing and vision loss. The attackers were arrested. Most got probation; one girl was sentenced to fifteen days in jail.

Today's teenagers tend to brag about being sexually promiscuous and being disrespectful. According to the Centers for Disease Control, nearly *half* of all high schoolers have had sexual intercourse.[14]

The disrespect among today's teens has even gone to violent extremes. One in three kids ages twelve through eighteen reports being bullied at school. One in five (21 percent) say they have been made fun of, 18 percent say they were the subject of rumors, and one in ten (11 percent) say they were tripped, shoved, or spat on.[15] You could call it the power of disrespect. As you will see, it is potent.

Like jackals in the jungle, bullies generally set their sights on the weak, ganging up on a child who's already dealing with some sort of issue that has led to a crisis of confidence. Sometimes it's a child with a learning disability or developmental issue. Other times the victim is physically different, either overweight or small for their grade. And usually the victims are boys on the cusp of puberty.

School counselor Jacques Savarèse told me that at the school where he's the guidance counselor, they can practically set their watches by the bullying behavior, it is so predictable. "Bullying rears its ugly head toward the end of fifth grade and the beginning of sixth grade," he said. "That coincides with the age of puberty, when I think there is an awakening of the mind. The kids, mostly boys, become more aware of what's in the news, what they hear at home, what they hear in the street. They start to get preconceived notions of the differences in human beings." The school meets with children several times during these critical years to specifically discuss the issue of bullying. The hope is to nip it in the bud before it ever becomes a problem. The antidote is for parents to encourage conversations about current events. Tap into what teens are talking about, and remind your child of the family values your family decided upon as discussed in chapter 2.

STICKS AND STONES
MAY BREAK MY BONES . . .

Fifth grade was when things started getting tough at school for Ryan Halligan. He'd been in special education classes his first years in school, getting help with some language and motor skills. By fifth grade, he was assessed ready to be mainstreamed. But Ryan's dad says his son wasn't as strong academically as most of the rest of the kids, and he had to work harder to keep up. One fellow fifth grader saw Ryan struggling, and he and his buddies picked on Ryan. But there were no physical threats. Ryan's family had him work with a therapist on coping skills, and by the end of the year, on the advice of the therapist, the sessions ended.

When Ryan entered middle school, the bullying resumed. After one tearful episode, Ryan's parents vowed to take it to the principal, but their son begged them not to. "That will only make it worse," he pleaded. Instead, Ryan asked to learn kickboxing so he could defend himself. Predictably, he got into a fight with his chief tormentor and "got a few good punches in," as Ryan put it, before a principal broke up the fight. It seemed the bullying had stopped. Time would tell how wrong that was.

A few weeks into Ryan's eighth-grade year, on October 7, 2003, Ryan hanged himself in the family bathroom. He was just thirteen. There was no suicide note, nothing to make sense of what had happened.

In John Halligan's search for clues to Ryan's suicide, he thumbed through his son's yearbook. The faces of kids who had bullied Ryan had been scribbled out. Next, Mr. Halligan logged onto Ryan's AOL account, and everything became clear. Instant messages revealed the vile and vicious things other students had said about Ryan. Web browsing history showed that Ryan had visited Web sites on pain-free suicide. When he mentioned to his AIM pals he was considering suicide, they encouraged him. "It's about time," one wrote. Ryan Halligan's online life had been a living hell, and no one in his family had the slightest idea.[16]

A victim of bullying is defined as a person "exposed, repeatedly over time, to negative actions on the part of one or more other students."[17] A survey of more than fifteen thousand sixth- to tenth-grade students found that the greatest number of victims were in sixth grade, as has been Mr. Savarèse's observation. The highest number of bullies are usually eighth graders.[18] This is the same age when children begin to actively separate from their parents, seeking more social acceptance and support from their peers instead of their parents. Forty-one percent of boys and 25 percent of girls in another study said they had actually been in a physical fight.[19] Fifty-three percent of boys and 37 percent of girls admitted to being bullies, with 12 percent of the boys saying it happens every week. Some experts believe bullying is done to show superiority and increase the bully's status in the eyes of his or her peers. Apparently it works. One review of fifth graders found that bullying increased their status and popularity within groups.[20] Another survey of sixth through eighth graders made a connection between boys described by the teachers as "aggressive and popular" and boys who were judged popular and "cool" by their peers.[21] We may not want to be bullies, but apparently kids do admire them.

If kids knew what becomes of bullies, they might not judge them "cool." Sixty percent of boys who were bullies in middle school end up with at least one criminal conviction by the age of twenty-four. Four in ten of them will have three or more convictions!

The impact on victims is significant. Kids who are bullied report having nearly three times as many headaches and twice as many sleep problems as children who are not bullied. They are also nearly twice as tense and three times as anxious.[22] As a result, kids who are bullied try to avoid school and have higher absentee rates.[23] It should come as no surprise that their grades are lower too.

Teachers like to think they're on top of this sort of thing. Unfortunately, they're not. In a study where 70 percent of the faculty state they intervene "almost all the time" when bullying occurs at their schools, the students say it's more like 25 percent of the time. Parents think they're doing the right thing, but there is a disconnect. Ninety-three percent of moms and dads say they've established strict Internet safety rules. Just over one-third of their kids agree with that, and 41 percent of children say their parents have no idea what they are doing online.[24]

In Ryan Halligan's tragic case, his family had clear rules about computer use and even knew Ryan's passwords. But Ryan never let on to the kind of vitriol that was being directed at him online. His parents had promised they'd never "snoop" at their children's messages. They were true to their word. It was only after Ryan killed himself that his family realized what was going on. "He was trying to manage the situation on his own," John Halligan said, adding, "A lot of these kids do, tragically."

It's gotten so bad there's a term for it: *bullycide*. When kids are tormented by relentless teasing, name calling, and insults, they sometimes see only one way out: death. Teen suicide rates are stunningly high. At present, it's estimated a young person tries to commit suicide every forty-two seconds. For every kid who's successful at taking his own life, another six survivors affected by that one death are considered at risk for taking their own lives.[25]

Could the Power of Respect decrease the likelihood of school-based and cyber bullying? There are a number of anti-bullying programs in schools around the country, and according to a review of the most prominent anti-bullying efforts, those that take a group approach in combating bullying do work.[26] The most effective way to change bullying behavior in children and adolescents is to stimulate in them a sense of self-awareness and get them talking about the impact of bullying.[27] Bringing teachers up to speed in recognizing bullying behavior is a key factor. As the statistic above notes, there is a wide gulf between what teachers think they know and what is really going on.

Currently, thirty-four states require schools to have anti-bullying policies. But having a policy and enforcing it are often two different things. In May 2008, Florida passed a tough anti-bullying law that puts school districts' funding on the line if they don't adopt effective policies discouraging in-person and online bullying. Florida is only the second state to impose financial penalties for noncompliance. The measure that passed is officially called the Jeffrey Johnston Stand Up for All Students Act, in memory of a popular, straight-A student who killed himself at age fifteen after two years of cyber bullying.

John Halligan has some advice for parents. He says, "Make sure you turn that computer off, often. Have a sit-down conversation about what is going on in your kids' lives. Create as much opportunity as you can to allow them to express their feelings and what they might be going through."

THE POWER OF RESPECT

Talk to your children about what is going on in their lives.

A TYPICAL DAY FOR TEENS

Imagine the typical day of an American high school teenager, Blake. Blake gets up at five thirty to cram for a test this morning. On the way to school, he'll grab a Starbucks and a Red Bull to get stoked for the day ahead. The school day begins with a flurry of classes, tests, and quick interchanges with friends in the hall during class change. Blake has a cross word with one of his friends, and that really nags at him when he heads off to his next class. While sitting in class, he's distracted by the argument and misses some of the critical notes he needed for the upcoming exam. Lunchtime arrives, and Blake's starved. But because he needs to make all-state band to burnish his college résumé, he grabs a power bar from his locker and heads to the rehearsal hall to get a half-hour lesson in.

After music, it's another blur of classes, during which two of the teachers strongly hint there will be a test the next day. After school, Blake runs to the sports center and changes for lacrosse practice. When practice is over, he grabs his backpack and heads over to the house of the eleven-year-old kid he's tutoring for math. By the time the tutoring lesson is over, it's eight o'clock. Blake drags himself through the door, plops down at the kitchen table, and pulls the foil off the plate of food his mother set aside for him. He's got about three hours of homework before he can even think about calling it a night.

That is a typical day. Add on the other baggage today's teens have, and it's enough to sidetrack even the most confident adult. Like adults, kids also get stressed from time pressures, and when they are, being respectful is not their top priority.

Take a look at some of what teens are having to confront. Today's kids are bombarded by pressures coming at them from every direction:

- Kids don't feel they have enough time to do what needs to be done during school hours. Students at a suburban New York high school were asked to account for how they spent their time outside of class. The result was an exhausting list of homework, after-school jobs, chores at home, sports commitments, and the like. It's easy to see why over the past twenty years, there's been a 12 percent loss in the amount of free time a child has, including a 25 percent drop in playtime and a 50 percent drop in outdoor activity.[28]

- Kids are burdened with high expectations from many directions. The pressure to get into a good college has resulted in the Kaplan test company enjoying revenues of $1.1 billion. Kids give up lunch periods to participate in that application-enhancing extracurricular that will help them get into the school they want. They pile on advanced-level classes where the homework load eats away even more at what little time kids have.

- Teens' bodies are changing, and they obsess over their body image. They report spending 4.3 hours each week in the gym.[29] Girls are three times more likely than boys to have a negative body image. Twelve percent of boys used potentially harmful products in the past year, like unregulated supplements and protein powders.[30]

- Pressures from the opposite sex aren't getting any easier. "Friends with benefits" is the solution to being sexually active with a member of the opposite sex without the complications of having an actual relationship. Two-thirds of college students responding to a survey said they have been in a "friends with benefits" relationship and said the main advantage was "no commitment."[31]

- Video images do impact teens. According to a study by Web MD, "Girls who viewed gangsta videos for at least fourteen hours per week were more likely to engage in negative behaviors. Fourteen hours is not that much. That's just two hours of 'background' noise a day. Over a one year study, they were three times more likely to hit a teacher, two and a half times more likely to get arrested, and twice as likely to have multiple sexual partners."[32]

- Kids risk becoming inured to messages of disrespect. A survey of two thousand urban teens recorded a shocking lack of respect for black women.[33] Six nouns were listed to refer to men, while fifteen were offered for women, all of them ugly. The attitudes behind the names speak to a devaluing of women and blasé attitudes. The study recommends "re-creating the social fabric" of these communities.

The environment in which teens are being raised *is* competitive, stressful, and not always respectful. Happily, the news about today's teens is not all bad because the Power of Respect sometimes does work its magic. In the next chapter, you will see the difference made when respect programs are introduced in schools. One Maryland high school student says, "I think we look at the student body differently. I definitely treat what used to be the renegade group differently. These students used to think they couldn't talk to me because they were going to get in trouble. Now, we will talk about what's going on in class or homecoming or something like that." That's the Power of Respect in relationships: finding common ground where it once appeared there was none.

Respect Reminders for Teens

☐ Determine your priorities.
☐ Develop a skill.
☐ Cultivate your support system of friends.
☐ Find your definition of success.
☐ Find someone who listens to you.

Respect Reminders for Parents

- [ ] Listen to your child.
- [ ] Be nonjudgmental.
- [ ] Talk about your family's definition of *respect*.
- [ ] Teach your child how to problem-solve.
- [ ] Appreciate your child's intellect.

Respect Reminders for Couples

- [ ] Listen, then talk.
- [ ] Consider the other person's needs.
- [ ] Fight fair.
- [ ] Acknowledge your spouse's efforts.
- [ ] Compliment your spouse.

4

Taming the Blackboard Jungle

The Power of Respect at School

Will was the kid whose name teachers cringed to see on their class list. *Oh no, not him!* was the thought each unlucky teacher had. Will was known as "big trouble" by just about everyone at his middle school. He acted up in class. He was all attitude and no action. After years of enduring Will's disruptions in whatever class he was assigned to, teachers were counting the days until he would be gone from the school. Will had been labeled "unteachable," and few instructors even bothered to try. Years of failure had proven that Will was a lost cause.

Pamela Carroll drew the short straw when Will entered eighth grade. By this point, Will was fifteen, tall, boisterous, and sullen when it came to participating in class. Ms. Carroll laughed as she recalled her initial reaction when she learned Will was in her class. "He had such a reputation I thought, *Oh, man! What am I gonna do?* I didn't think I was going to be a hero, but you do want to see every one of them succeed. Yet Will was a real challenge. What was I going to do with this child, given what he brought to the classroom?"

What Ms. Carroll knew about Will's life outside school wasn't very encouraging. "I think that is one of the things we are getting wrong in education," she said. "We focus on what is going on in the classroom and even within the school, and we forget that these kids bring their whole world wrapped around them." Will's world was pretty tough. He lived on the rough side of town where drugs and drive-by shootings were an everyday occurrence. He seemed to get himself to school. As far as she knew, no one had ever attended a parent-teacher conference to talk about Will. No one seemed to care about Will, so he didn't care about himself either.

But his eighth-grade teacher soldiered on, determined not to let this young man derail her lesson plans, wondering if somehow she could get through to him.

One of Ms. Carroll's first projects for her class was a "directed individualized reading project." Kids would choose a book to read over a two-week period and would create some sort of presentation about it for the class. It could be a written report, dramatic reenactment, or some sort of artistic or graphic project. Before the project began, Ms. Carroll wanted to get a sense of what kind of reading her students had done. "I asked them to write a list of the books they had read in the last two years and their all-time favorites . . . and to describe themselves as readers."

When she collected the students' folders, one stood out. Across the top of Will's folder was only this, in a scraggly line: "*i don't read i won't read i can't read*." The teacher stopped cold. Now it all made sense. Of *course* Will acted up in class and put on a tough front. He was illiterate. For eight years, he'd been passed from class to class, tolerated but not taught. No wonder he pretended not to care about school. There was nothing in it for him. Besides, who would want to admit he was "dumb," especially a fifteen-year-old boy?

Ms. Carroll recalls, "I made a deal with Will. He and I talked about what kind of movies and stories he liked, and I discovered he was really into adventure and mystery." With that interest as a possible entry point, the teacher racked her brain trying to figure out how she could help him. "I found some books on tape and the corresponding print texts at the public library," she explained. "Working with a graduate assistant, Will sat and 'read' the stories and several of the books, using the tapes to support him as he followed along in the text version." Together, the teacher and the struggling student came up with a way for Will to "save face" as he struggled to learn to read. "He pretended to be listening to music, bouncing his head to an imaginary beat so that no one would know what he was up to." Within a few days, Will was arriving early to class, settling into his seat with his tape player and books, and getting started even before Ms. Carroll was ready for him.

It was an encouraging start, but the real test was yet to come: the presentation. Like the other kids, Will had signed up for a slot to present his project, but would he actually do it?

"I was afraid that Will would revert to his normal antics, the tough guy who values snarling but not schooling," Ms. Carroll recalled. "But to my surprise, he got to the classroom by seven o'clock with a poster rolled up under his arm. He had ridden his bike from the rough side of town early in the morning so he could be sure to find a safe place to keep the project until class."

Will went on to make a presentation on Sir Arthur Conan Doyle's short story "The Adventure of the Speckled Band," complete with a poster visual and the introduction of new vocabulary words to his classmates. His effort was appreciated by everyone, and the class gave him enthusiastic applause for his work.

"*Never* before had Will ever participated in class in a positive way," Ms. Carroll told me emphatically. "It was an unbelievable first, especially considering Will was fifteen years old. But this time, he had done the work and was proud to show the results."

This was a critical turning point for Will. Most people would have given up on this teenager from the "bad" side of town—and indeed, most everyone at Will's school had. But this one teacher, unwilling to let this boy go down without fighting for him, found a way to connect with him. The touch point was respect. Ms. Carroll's strategy of using audiobooks to support Will's reading efforts did not belittle him for his illiteracy but offered a solution. Pretending to bop along to music gave Will the ability to not lose respect around his classmates. It was the cover he needed to look cool while doing his remedial work.

Instead of writing him off, his teacher became interested enough in Will to see what made him tick. It may well have been the first time anyone ever asked Will what *he* thought about things. She had a simple conversation that to Will's thinking revealed that someone at school was actually interested in *him*. This is one of the straightforward uses of the Power of Respect, one of the most easily practiced, yet also one of the most easy to avoid.

"It's one of the really simple things that works. Give students choices," Carroll says. Working with adolescents, the educator has found that a critical way of using the Power of Respect to motivate her students is in offering them choices. "Help them learn how to make choices. 'Do you want to do this project or this project to show you have learned the content?'" she says. "Choices are huge for adolescents when they are on the cusp between being children or being adults. They want choices, but they need fences. They need adults to guide them."

What should those fences look like to assure kids' success in school? Experts recommend a number of strategies: help students set their own goals, set high expectations for students, involve students in the evaluation process, use a variety of approaches in teaching, encourage students to keep trying, and teach social skills when assigning cooperative tasks.[1] When kids know where they stand, know what is expected of them, and are given tools to help achieve it, their chances of success increase.

THE POWER OF RESPECT
*When kids know what is expected of them,
their chances of success increase.*

WHEN CLASSROOMS ARE CHAOS

That's all fine and good when life in the classroom is calm. But what if the academic environment is completely chaotic? Here's a snapshot of daily life in way too many schools in America, straight from teachers themselves.

- "I once saw a student eat an entire rotisserie chicken, a tub of mashed potatoes with gravy, and a two-liter Pepsi in the back of my class. He did try to belch quietly."[2]
- "Aside from the two exam days, she never came to class. Her term paper was three weeks late. Then she complained when I gave her a B–."[3]
- "I caught him red-handed with a term paper plagiarized from the Internet. He was so lazy he forgot to delete the real author's name from the last page."[4]

And then there are the everyday incidents. Some make the news; most don't.

- A fourteen-year-old girl who refused to stop texting on her cell phone is arrested by Wauwatosa, Wisconsin, police.[5]
- A group of eighth-grade boys taunt their language teacher, using the high-pitched hum of a cell phone. His older ears can't hear it, but the students in class can. The

veteran educator has no idea why they are snickering,
but he knows the kids are up to something.

It's asking a lot of a teacher to maintain a classroom of respect when it seems so little of it is being directed their way. Across the country, teachers complain of rowdy, disrespectful children who bully one another and talk out of turn in class. Parents and kids agree that children are bringing the disrespectful culture of the world around them into the classroom daily.[6] Safety is one concern. Half of the teachers in America say their school has an armed guard.[7] Eighty-six percent of public schools reported at least one violent incident in the 2005–2006 school year, including fourteen homicides.[8] It's hard to teach a class when you or your students are worried about getting hurt.

The bigger concern, however, is discipline. The discipline problems that teachers and parents say descend from a culture of disrespect take valuable time away from teaching, and students are losing out as a result. Three out of four teachers say they could be much more effective if it weren't for discipline problems from students disrupting class by talking out or goofing off. That's followed by disrespecting the teacher, cheating, showing up late, bullying, and being rowdy outside of the classroom, like in the lunchroom or hallways. The storm clouds created by this kind of behavior make it a daunting, if not impossible, challenge to teach.

The good news is—it's *not* the majority of kids in a class who are causing all the trouble. It's usually the same kids over and over again. But as one teacher puts it, "One kid can blow up an entire class." How? As the teacher explains, in her class, there are three kinds of students: the ones who are prepared and eager and ready to learn, the disruptive troublemakers who have no interest in school, and the large "swing vote" of students who could go either way. Depending on which way the swing vote students lean, an entire class can lose out because of one rowdy classmate.

The eighth-grade boys in Mr. Herbert's class knew they were having a poetry quiz that morning. They were chattering as they arrived, bumping into desks and moving into the classroom with the usual shuffling and clumsiness of fourteen-year-old boys. Mr. Herbert called over the noise, "Take your seats, gentlemen.

> He who walks with wise men will be wise, but the companion of fools will be destroyed.
> —PROVERBS 13:20

You'll need the entire class period for today's quiz." A few groans could be heard as bodies were flung into their seats. The teacher walked around the room, handing out the test to each boy.

As the kids looked at the test, a few moaned, "You are kidding, right?" Something on the test sheet must have looked too difficult.

"I never joke about poetry," Mr. Herbert said brusquely. "You boys know that."

Soon the class was mostly silent, but for the scratching of pencils on paper. But not for long. "What's a viceroy?" called out one boy at about the same time another student got up and lumbered over to the electric pencil sharpener.

"That's a representative of the king," Mr. Herbert explained. "Sort of like his stand-in." "This is nuts," a boy in the corner complained about the test, as he ran his hands through his hair in frustration. Among other things, the quiz asked boys to analyze a poem, giving its meaning and identifying the poem's meter. Another child called out, "We've never seen these words before—*fey?*"

Mr. Herbert replied, "That's an old-fashioned way of saying 'happily.'" Two more kids were now loudly sharpening their pencils. On the back row, one boy reached over to his neighbor's desk and took a pencil. "Yours is sharper than mine," he said loudly.

"What the heck is a viceroy?" came the call from another student.

The definition was again provided by the teacher, as it would be at least twice more before the test was done. "C'mon, guys!" one boy shouted in apparent frustration over the noise level during the test.

THE POWER OF RESPECT

The tone of the classroom is critical to learning.

> "I am tired of beating my head against the wall. I feel like my principal won't deal with the discipline problems here and is actually angry when we send a kid to admin."
>
> —JENNIFER, A HIGH SCHOOL TEACHER

Children of this age often have procedural questions during tests. Only once did the classroom visitor, who was sitting just out of view, see a student approach the teacher's desk to ask a question. Over and again students called out in class.

The tone of the classroom is critical to learning. A respectful classroom is a place "where all students feel physically and emotionally safe and valued for who they are. Students who do not feel safe and valued will find it impossible to focus on academics or relationships with others."[9] One could add that teachers need to feel valued as well, in order to best do what they are trained to do—teach.

A Respectful Classroom . . .
- Has rules everyone has helped draft.
- Has students and teachers who use respectful words.

- Has quiet voices and bodies.
- Is a place where students listen to the teacher and to other students.
- Is a learning environment where everyone is polite.
- Sets high expectations for students.
- Has students who come to class prepared.

LACK OF RESPECT FOR TEACHERS

Many teachers in America say they are overworked, underpaid, and underappreciated. Teachers usually enter the profession for the joy of teaching, not the salary. Eight out of ten teachers in one survey say they wanted to make a difference for children and society; seven out of ten were motivated by working with children or adolescents; and the same number report it was their passion for teaching. Nearly two-thirds of first-year teachers felt a calling to the teaching profession.[10] After five years on the job, 50 percent of them are gone. Why?

There are many reasons cited by teachers for leaving schools, but you can boil it down to one phrase: lack of respect. Defiance and disrespect count for the most trips to the principal's office.[11] Countless surveys list lack of support, bad behavior by students, too much to do without the necessary resources, and little input in the bureaucratic requirements that seem to constantly increase. Bombarded by rowdy students and frustrated by the sense that they

> It's gotten to the point that it is so bad, I've called the local employment office to see about another kind of job.
>
> —FRUSTRATED TEACHER

are completely on their own, with no support and no backup, teachers who entered the profession for altruistic reasons are leaving it disheartened and disappointed. At the current rate of attrition, fully half of the teachers in classrooms today will someday be doing something else professionally.

Says one teacher, "I would want to work in a school where my special skills and talents are appreciated; where fellow teachers are positive, empathetic, and supportive; where the principal values the needs of parents just as much as those of the teachers because he understands that a healthy positive learning environment for students requires mutual respect and collaboration among all relevant parties. I would still be teaching today if these conditions existed when I taught."[12]

Could creating a culture of respect in schools change that attrition rate? If the Power of Respect were practiced in our schools, would the teacher quoted above have stayed in the profession? Would the students have behaved better?

Outside the classroom, more than three in four kids say they frequently hear swearing in the halls and cafeteria (also the source of most school discipline reports). Almost half in big schools and a third in smaller schools see a fight at least once a month and a third say there is a serious problem with bullying.

THE POWER OF RESPECT

The Power of Respect in schools
reduces discipline problems and helps kids learn.

In Louisiana, things got so bad that a law was actually made requiring respect in schools. In 1999, the state legislature passed the nation's first "manners law,"[13] requiring all schoolchildren to refer to teachers, administrators, and other school workers as "sir" or "ma'am." The wife of the bill's sponsor, Don Cravins, was a public schoolteacher who'd quit in disgust over parents' failure to discipline their children. Cravins said at the time of passage, "The lack of respect in and out of school is a national problem."

The Power of Respect can be a powerful solution to the problem of school rudeness and rowdiness—and it doesn't require an act of Congress to make it happen.

A Fourth "R"—Reading, Writing, 'Rithmetic, and Respect

When schools embrace an attitude that puts an emphasis on respect, spelling out acceptable behavior and the responsibilities that go along with being a student, there is a measurable improvement in conduct as well as academics—and teachers are reinvigorated in their profession.

THE POWER OF RESPECT
The Power of Respect can be a huge motivator in schools.

Here's what's been happening at schools in Maryland where a program emphasizing respect began a decade ago. The number of kids being sent to the office for disciplinary reasons dropped significantly. Schools with this program, emphasizing the Power of Respect, had 35 percent fewer kids getting Office Disciplinary Reports than is the case nationally. If each referral takes about forty-five minutes of teacher and administrator time, that's a savings of 139 hours of instructional time or seventeen days! You can teach a child a lot in seventeen days. The percentage of kids getting suspended declined significantly compared to schools without respect programs.

Most exciting, children are learning. At one elementary school in Philadelphia, three years after a behavior program was implemented,

82.2 percent of third graders were passing their reading tests, compared to just 44.3 percent before the program began. In Baltimore County Public Schools, where reading and math scores have been on the rise, they are rising faster at schools with respect programs. Third graders increased their reading proficiency by 46 percent compared to 33 percent at schools without the program. Eighth graders saw their math scores increase by 79 percent compared to a 42-percent jump elsewhere.[14] Scores are up because the time freed for teaching is enormous. Kids in schools with respect programs are 40 percent less likely to need counseling for inappropriate behavior and 34 percent less likely to need counseling for social skills. They are picking up on the right way to behave because they see it modeled and reinforced all around them. There is also evidence to suggest that the de-charged atmosphere of a school with respect programs has ancillary benefits for its most challenged students. Boys who begin their schooling where respect programs are already in place were 38 percent less likely to receive special education services and were 27 percent less likely to be referred for special education assessment.[15] The sooner kids are exposed to the Power of Respect, the better.

> Respect your efforts, respect yourself. Self-respect leads to self-discipline. When you have both firmly under your belt, that's real power.
>
> —CLINT EASTWOOD

BRINGING RESPECT BACK TO SCHOOLS

Thanks to the inspirational leadership of Adam Sheinhorn, kids at North County High School in Glen Burnie, Maryland, like going to school a lot more. So do their teachers.

Six years ago, Sheinhorn was a newly appointed assistant principal at North County High, which was a disaster in the discipline department. Things had gotten so out of hand that the school on occasion was put on lockdown because of violent outbreaks between students. It was a stressful place both for students who wanted to learn and teachers who were just trying to do their job. The minute the bell rang, everyone who could leave, did.

Then Sheinhorn brought the Power of Respect to the school. At a countywide education meeting, he heard of something called PBIS, Positive Behavioral Interventions and Supports, which other schools credited for incredible improvements in rowdy schools. The assistant principal found out that the two middle schools that fed into the high school used PBIS, so it seemed natural to have it at North County High.

His principal threw cold water on the idea. They'd been there, done that. Sheinhorn told me, "She tried to present it to the faculty, and the reception was very negative. I then learned the way it was presented was as a directive: 'We're going to do it, and you have no say.' So of course, it fell on its face." Sheinhorn asked if he could give it another try.

This time, the teachers, facilitated by Sheinhorn, talked about the possibilities. They were part of the decision-making process, deciding what strategies to consider, what they hoped to achieve with the program. "A lot of it is self-reflection, which is not something you get to do often," Sheinhorn explained. "It wasn't something else to do, but it got you back to your roots and reminded you why you got into the teaching profession in the first place: because you care about kids and you want to do what good people do for one another." The transformation at North County High has been nothing short of stunning, thanks to the program Sheinhorn shepherded into the school.

The school developed what it calls the "Knight's Code," named for the school mascot. It is "We respect ourselves, others, learning, and property." Sheinhorn says teachers and students spent a lot of time discussing what that means. He explained, "We talk about working hard for yourself and having integrity. We talk about feeling good about yourself and having confidence and not caving in to peer pressure. We discuss respecting others, not judging someone or putting pressure on someone to do something. With learning and property," he continued, "you respect the effort that everyone is making. You respect your school and have pride in it and work as hard as you can to be successful in school."

The results are evident across the board. North County used to expel about fifty-six kids every year. Today, the figure is a fraction of that. Teachers used to come and go like a revolving door. Now no one leaves their teaching position unless they're having a baby or returning to college. The school has seen a 30-percent increase in its pass rate on the state's standardized English test. But if you really want to know if North County High has changed, ask a child who goes there.

"Chaotic." That's the word Rebecca Stolzenbach chooses to describe North County High School when she was a freshman. "We had fights all the time. There would be fights in the hallway and fights in the parking lot. I still remember we had a riot in the back parking lot with close to forty students. The school was on lockdown for the rest of the day. It was bad that year." Now a senior, Rebecca looks back with amazement at how radically her school has changed.

One of the key changes Rebecca singles out is the consistency with which discipline is handled. "The administration, teachers, and faculty are all on the same page," she told me. "Before, students knew which administrators to go to so they could get out of trouble. Now there is no picking and choosing. You have to face the consequences of your actions." But the consequences of good behavior can be pretty appealing.

Teachers and administrators hand out "Knight's Notes" whenever they see a student particularly exemplifying the code of the school. The Knight's Notes can then be traded in for tangible benefits like pencils or, extremely popular, access to the school stores where snacks are sold. Rebecca told me that on days when the school store is open, the line stretches around the corner of the building. Everyone in it has earned the right to be there because they have exhibited the Power of Respect.

In the halls, Rebecca says the Power of Respect means walls are no longer marked up, lockers aren't vandalized, and kids have a sense of pride in their school. But Rebecca gets most excited when she talks about the change in one student who'd been the same sort of behavior problem as Will, mentioned earlier in this chapter. When PBIS was implemented, it was discovered this boy read on only a fourth-grade level. He wasn't a behavior problem after all. His issues were academic. What happened next is a testament to the Power of Respect generated by PBIS.

"A teacher took his only planning period and went through reading with him," Rebecca told me. "Now he is reading on a ninth-grade level. He's in school every day. He's not skipping class. I have seen firsthand that it works!"

Susan Barrett, a former teacher and administrator, has been co-coordinator of the Maryland PBIS initiative for more than a decade. At the vanguard of an effort to change a disruptive school environment from a place of inconsistent, punishing policies to a place where kids can learn and educators can teach, Barrett and the state leadership team focused on implementing preventive strategies in schools, with the goal of making schools less chaotic by improving students' behavior through targeted actions by teachers and staff. First implemented in Oregon, Hawaii, Illinois, and Maryland, PBIS is now in nine thousand schools, and thirty-one states across the country are working on the program.

One would hope respect and positive behavior would not need to be taught in schools, but experience has shown that too many children at school simply don't know the proper way to interact with others—and they often infect the other children who do. The word *infect* is critical here, because the team took a lot of its cues in fighting disruptive behavior from the public health model. If you want to vaccinate against a disease, inoculate the entire population and then give special treatment to the few who still show symptoms of the ailment.

PBIS is not a specific curriculum or practice but rather a decision-making framework designed to improve student behavior and academic outcomes. It focuses on ensuring that all students have access to the most effective and accurate instructional and behavioral practices and interventions possible. This "system" approach seems to be working. The strategy lets go of any notion that kids know what it means to be respectful. It's a disheartening realization, to be sure, but Barrett says it's critical. "We make a lot of assumptions about kids' knowledge when they walk into a school, but we can't assume they know what respect looks like," she explains. You have to teach it just like any other skill. She continues, "Just like we provide feedback for skill development in math or reading, we have to apply the same instructional logic for social skills. We want to be sure we are providing the same feedback on the social skills side."

The implementation of PBIS is school specific. Positive behavior intervention works, Barrett told me, because the schools themselves decide what kind of culture they'd like to see by compiling a simple list of three to five expectations they'd like to see met in their school. Administrators, staff, and teachers collectively decide what respect looks like in their school, and with the guidance of PBIS counselors, each school designs its own blueprint with a defined target of the kind of school culture and behavior desired, specifics on how that culture will be communicated to the students and staff, rewards to recognize positive behavior, and regular data collection so everyone knows where the school is in meeting its goal. Two components are critical to success: everyone must buy into the idea, and the message and practices must be consistent schoolwide.

"We are not going to go into a school and dictate what respect looks like for them. It is based on their unique needs, challenges, student and staff characteristics. Their school community can develop practices and procedures that fit their school context," says Barrett. You can usually identify a school with a respect program in place the minute you walk in. You might walk over a welcome mat that says, "Be Safe. Be Kind. Be a Positive Learner" as you do at Westwood Elementary. At McCormick Elementary in Maryland, kids make posters to "Strive for Five: be respectful, be safe, work peacefully, strive for excellence, and follow directions."

THE POWER OF RESPECT
Define the behavior you want to see.

Barrett says each school tries to find as many ways to repeat their target goals as possible. "You will see posters in our schools that say be respectful, be responsible, be ready to learn. Well, what does that look like and sound like, and how does that vary from setting to setting? It looks like this in this classroom: We keep our sounds low. We are prepared for class. We bring our homework. Then we go to the hallway, and we say, 'You keep your hands to yourself, you walk in a single-file line, you keep your sounds low.'" Teachers are generally given great latitude in translating the school's core values to their students, a welcome change in an educational landscape overrun with dictates from the district level and higher that frequently frustrate creative teaching practices.

Once a school decides what its values theme will be, teachers present the theme to the students and get their input on how to implement it. For example, if a school's goal is "respect, responsible, and ready to learn," PBIS Behavior Counselors or Behavior Support Coaches encourage teachers to get their classes to define how best to achieve it. That is vital, considering three-quarters of teachers who stay in the profession say having appropriate authority over curriculum is a key reason they're still teaching.[16] "You need to get buy-in ownership of this," said Barrett. "Conduct a class meeting and ask the students, 'What is it we expect from one another? What do we expect out of this classroom?' The students help to establish the rules, based on the matrix you've established for the entire school."

When a new academic or social skill is introduced, it is important to provide feedback, and initially schools use tangible rewards to students when they perform. Having students weigh in on what those rewards might be is important. What might motivate the teacher could be completely unimpressive to a child.

THE POWER OF RESPECT

Encourage the Power of Respect with rewards for good behavior.

North County High School uses "Knight's Notes," but the acknowledgments could be something as simple as "gotcha tickets" that are handed out when a child is demonstrating politeness or showing respect for others. Stickers and gold stars that can add up to a small prize are useful. Some teachers form paper chains from the ceiling to the floor. Each time a student meets the school's target goals, a link is added to the chain with a popcorn party reward when the chain reaches the floor. At the high school level, the reward could be access to the snacks store, preferred parking at school, or reduced fees on prom tickets or for sporting events. The reward needn't (and shouldn't) be grand—just a tangible acknowledgment of the child's successful effort. The external rewards are recommended *only* during the initial implementation of the program or when the behavior data shows a need for improvement. Barrett recommends a ratio of five positive acknowledgments for every correction in behavior. "Rather than point out what they are not doing well, you want to reinforce what they are doing well." She tells teachers to point out the students' mistakes when they don't act appropriately but be sure to acknowledge the desired behavior when it does happen.

Kids also need to see the adults model the appropriate behavior throughout the school day. Barrett says, "When the kids arrive in the morning, greet them and say, 'I'm really glad you're here.' But make sure it is authentic because kids know when you're faking it. Or say, 'You got work in on time. I really appreciate that.' It becomes embedded into the natural flow of conversation. When the behavior doesn't meet expectations, point it out, but also let them know what to do instead: 'Yesterday we had a lot of little interruptions during class. Please make sure you raise your hand when you need my attention.'"

Modeling and rewarding desired behavior is a critical component of PBIS. But it's the dialogue and interaction between teacher and pupils that seem to have the greatest impact. The hierarchy of education understandably puts teachers and administrators in a superior position to their students. But a common refrain among students, especially those deemed underachievers, is that teachers "talk down" to them. Remember Will, the eighth grader whose teacher discovered he couldn't read? To administrators at middle school, he was a recalcitrant boy who had no respect for teachers or the rules. It's understandable why no teacher had ever reached out to Will—based on his behavior, he didn't deserve it. He got lucky when he was assigned to Ms. Carroll's class.

The evidence is persuasive that giving teachers leeway in the classroom and a say in how the school's value system will be implemented is benefiting students. Teachers seem to be benefiting as well. With less time being wasted on office visits and detention, teachers have gotten back more class time with their students.

At North County High School this year, when graduating seniors leave for the last time, it will be with an emotion not seen at this school for a very long time: regret. Rebecca Stolzenbach told me, "You have no idea. About a week ago, it hit me. I'm leaving this place and from then on, I will only be a visitor. I almost started crying!"

Four years ago, Rebecca was among those who couldn't wait to get off campus at the end of the day. Isn't it incredible that the Power of Respect could actually make a teenager *want* to be at school?

TEACHING WITH RESPECT

Pamela Carroll no longer teaches in middle school. Today she is an associate dean at Florida State University. She still lays down the law with her university students just as she did when she taught middle and high school students. "I start out the year by saying something like this: 'I will respect you by doing these things. I will never show up without being well prepared, and I expect the same of you. I will read your work carefully with my best ideas and my best suggestions and criticisms and hope it is helpful.' I tell them explicitly what I mean by respect." With emphasis she adds, "I say, 'Because I treat you with respect, I expect respect back.' And it works! It really works."

THE POWER OF RESPECT
Treat people with respect, and expect respect back.

Students like Will, who have teachers who make an effort to connect as Ms. Carroll did, are likely to become academic success stories, even when the child's previous history has been so lackluster. The motivating style of a teacher can be critical in this regard.

Students who have supportive teachers like Ms. Carroll are more likely to stay in school,[17] do better in class,[18] be more creative,[19] and be more emotionally positive.[20] Schools that foster an environment of respect and responsibility have a greater likelihood of making that happen.

THE LASTING EFFECTS OF RESPECT

Middle school teacher Susan Ward tries to demonstrate respect for her students. With more than twenty years of teaching experience, Mrs. Ward has seen it all but still enjoys being a teacher and connecting with her students. If her students are in a play, Mrs. Ward is in the audience. "I cannot tell you how many times I have seen the *Nutcracker*. I know it by heart now," she said during our interview. "I do it because I care about them. When you get kids to understand that you care about them, they will listen to what you have to say." Two days after Mrs. Ward and I talked, she slept outside in refrigerator boxes with a group of high school kids, raising money and awareness about the homeless. She really lives her job of letting kids know she cares what they're doing!

Usually Mrs. Ward teaches gifted middle school students. But recently she was asked to take on a class of underachievers, older than most of their classmates because their academic failures had kept them back in school. "Several had never experienced success in school," Mrs. Ward recalled. "And they were nervous because they knew I taught the really smart kids, and they didn't know how it would be in my class. To be honest, I was also kind of nervous about dealing with kids who were so unmotivated."

Mrs. Ward decided to keep her usual high expectations for this class. "I told them I knew they were not in the gifted program, but I thought they could be if they tried really hard. I said that since I'm the teacher of the smart kids, I am the best teacher for you to be with, and we took it from there." It was not the easiest year in this veteran teacher's career, but it may have been one of the more fulfilling she's had at the school where kids are so at risk for dropping out, there is actually a coach to encourage these middle schoolers to hang in there until high school. Another coach plays the same role to keep high school students from dropping out.

Mrs. Ward says there were a few days when the grammar lesson got short shrift. "I was talking to them about life lessons. I told them they have to take care of themselves and stand up for themselves. We talked about what was right or wrong." She continued with passion in her voice, "There is a whole litany of things you have to talk with kids about, because either they're not getting it at home, or it's not sinking in."

The conversations had impact. At the close of that challenging school year, Mrs. Ward did her usual outplacement interview with her students. "I do that each year. I ask them for their feedback on what went well that year, what lesson they particularly enjoyed or learned the most from, or even which one I should scrap." Their response was not what she expected. "I was shocked to hear one of them say (and others echoed) that what had made the year a success for them was that I treated them like they mattered. They said that I never talked down to them, and that I talked with them, not at them."

THE POWER OF RESPECT
Teachers who respect students talk with them, not at them.

The new approach may have impacted these seventh graders academically. After receiving the feedback from her students, Mrs. Ward took a look at that year's standardized testing scores. "I had kids pass for the first time ever. The *first* time they *ever* passed the state testing! One student went up to almost exceeding the target."

Mrs. Ward can't help but believe it was the Power of Respect that came from those kids feeling valued in class. "I realized once again how important words are and how effective they can be. I try to always remember to use respect as a positive tool, especially with kids who feel like they don't matter in most other places."

What about the students lucky enough to have a teacher familiar with the Power of Respect? Laura was one of Mrs. Ward's eighth-grade students four years ago. Her senior year in high school, she wrote Mrs. Ward a letter, which reads in part:

Dear Mrs. Ward,

I know you may not remember me, that I may have been just another one of your students. First of all, allow me to introduce myself. I was one of your students about four years ago. It's been a long time, but I just wanted to take the time to tell you the huge impact you have had in my life. I remember the very first day I walked into your classroom. You made me feel so comfortable. Sitting in your room was like being surrounded by my friends.

Thanks to you, I became a much better writer and now I actually enjoy writing. The two years of English I had with you were, I think, the two best of my life. How can I forget the last day of my eighth grade year? You called me to your room and gave me a hug. You said that I would forget you, but as you can see, I never did. Now that I am about to graduate, I wanted to let you know how much I appreciate having had you as a teacher. You taught me that I can always improve and never to settle for less than my best. There are not enough words to express how much your teachings have influenced me.

Although you may still not remember who I am, it is okay for I will always remember who you are.

Sincerely,
Laura

Mrs. Ward *did* remember Laura, even before she got the letter. Now she's sure she will never forget her.

Respect Reminders

—————————— ✑ ——————————

☐ Take an interest and show you care.
☐ Give kids controlled choices.
☐ Spell out what respect means with input from everyone.
☐ Reward desired behavior.

5

The Best Business Tool—and It's Free!

The Power of Respect in Business

It was a typical day in the food preparation area of a Nashville Kentucky Fried Chicken restaurant. In less than an hour, the lunchtime rush would begin, with hungry customers lining up for sacks of the nation's most popular take-out chicken. Colonel Sanders's recipe for "Finger Lickin' Good" chicken might be a secret, but the key to making customers happy was not. The food had to be hot, fresh, and served quickly as orders came in. Twenty minutes was as long as a piece of chicken could sit under the warming lamps. Any longer, and the crust would go soggy. The kitchen had to run with the precision of a space launch.

As Peter Georgescu, former chairman and chief executive officer of the advertising firm Young and Rubicam, retells the story in his memoir, *The Source of Success*, he and his partner John McGarry were working like crazy in the restaurant's kitchen. They'd been cooking chicken, chopping coleslaw, and buttering corn. They'd swept the floors and changed the lights and served the customers. Three days into the gig, they'd learned the differences between

107

preparing original recipe and extra crispy. And they were dog tired. As Georgescu recalls, he didn't even have the energy for a conversation over a beer at the end of the workday.

It was a far cry from their usual day job, which generally found them in the plush offices of Young and Rubicam, one of the nation's top advertising agencies. McGarry and Georgescu weren't cooking chicken to learn a new trade; they were getting ready for an advertising war.

The advertising world's shootout is pretty much everything the name suggests—a fight to the death, victory to the last man standing. The Kentucky Fried Chicken account, one of the biggest in the nation at the time, was up for grabs, and the team at Young and Rubicam ("Y&R") was desperate to win it. The ad men working in Tennessee were doing reconnaissance, learning how the restaurant worked from the fry station up. As Georgescu tells the story, when the time came to present Y&R's concept for the new KFC advertising campaign, they wowed the restaurant executives with their creative work and knowledge of the business. Then a question came up: "If the original recipe is so good," the KFC man asked, "why not use it on the extra crispy?" The room was quiet. Finally, Georgescu told them it wasn't possible. "The key to original recipe is the pressure cooking," he explained. Only someone who'd spent time in the Kentucky Fried Chicken kitchen would understand that distinction. The opposing agencies never knew what hit them. Y&R got the account.[1]

Most advertising executives look at that story and admire the creative way the Y&R team went after a lucrative account. No question, their approach *was* clever. But to the executives at Kentucky Fried Chicken, it was much more than that. The Y&R move had changed the calculus in the decision-making process from "Who has the better ideas?" to "Which agency do we want to work with?" The Madison Avenue team with the clever tagline—or the group who cared enough about what we do to put on an apron and get sweaty frying chicken?

For the executives at Kentucky Fried Chicken, the decision was a no-brainer: they chose to go with the people who *respected* their business enough to find out everything they could about it. The Y&R team's investment of time and thought beyond the routine preparation for a campaign pitch stood out to the client. By learning about the restaurant's business from the kitchen up, the Y&R team telegraphed that it understood the nuance of what made the product unique. It also assured that if the advertising message ever needed to be quickly massaged, the Y&R group could reasonably be assumed to be up to the job.

The Power of Respect in Business

Nowhere is the boomerang effect of respect more measurable than in business. Whether it's reaching out for new customers or protecting the business you already have, the Power of Respect is potent. It can motivate employees to work more productively and enhance their creativity. It can eliminate employee turnover and expensive training of new hires. It can solidify and help build existing customer relationships, adding to a firm's bottom line.

THE POWER OF RESPECT
The Power of Respect can add to a firm's bottom line.

One of the key indicators for a business's future success is the degree to which it innovates. It's no surprise that many of the top ten most admired companies in the annual *Fortune* magazine survey are also tops in innovation. Apple ranked number one in both overall admiration as well as innovation. Anyone with an iPod or iPhone will understand why. Google ranked number four overall. Its "Do No Evil" motto encourages employees to strategize ways to do more with the Web. Workers at Google feel respected by the autonomy they are given to pursue business ideas that might not be part of their particular job description. Engineers at Google are given 20 percent of their time to spend working on something they are passionate about.[2] Google Scholar was created this way. Two engineers who had been working on building Google's Web index decided to use some sabbatical time to index scholarly articles, much to the delight of anyone trying to do some quick research.

At 3M, the company encourages employees to follow their ideas, even if the innovations are not connected to their segment's line of business. In 1968, a 3M researcher named Spencer Silver was experimenting with various adhesives. He developed something that stuck but didn't leave a film. It was an interesting discovery, but no one could find any particular use for it because it wasn't "sticky enough." It was relegated to the "failed products" pile.

> If it were easy,
> someone else
> would do it.
> —ART FRY,
> INVENTOR
> OF POST-IT
> NOTES

Six years later, Art Fry, a new products developer at 3M, was singing in the church choir. He was frustrated that his bookmarks kept falling out of the hymnal. The sermon was dull and he kept thinking about his bookmark problem. For whatever reason, he recalled that slightly sticky adhesive and figured it might hold a slip of paper without damaging the page. He went to the lab and made up some samples. It was the beginning of Post-it notes and a revolution in office products.[3]

Innovation isn't easy, but it *is* essential. Business leaders across the country would argue that innovation is critical to any successful company's growth and success. How can the Power of Respect play a role in innovation? To understand the connection, let's look at the relation between employee positivity, creativity, and job performance.

DEVELOP A POSITIVE COMPANY CULTURE

People who are in a positive mood think better. It's not that they are necessarily smarter, but their minds are more flexible and better equipped to find connections between seemingly unrelated items. People who feel good are more able to suspend long-held impressions and be open to other possibilities. Dr. Alice Isen of Cornell University has spent more than thirty years studying this phenomenon and is a leading expert on *positive affect*—or "feeling good." Through a variety of experiments, Isen has proved that when people experience positive emotions, they are more creative and elastic in their thinking, coming up with unusual but sensible ways of categorizing information. Relationships and associations can be made between items that on first glance seem totally disconnected.

Isen proved this in an experiment in which one group of participants were first put in a positive mood by receiving a small, inexpensive gift.[4] A control group got nothing. Then the volunteers were asked to make associations between certain words. Here's an example:

1. What one word links these three words together?
   Cottage, Blue, Mouse
2. What one word links these three words together?
   Atomic, Mower, Foreign

The experiment illustrated how feeling good can change your thinking. The answers to the questions above are in the endnotes.[5] You may not have correctly guessed the answers, but once you see what they are, they make complete sense. In countless other experiments, the link between clarity of thinking and positive mood has been definitely made.

Here's how it works. When you are feeling positive, your brain releases dopamine, the feel-good hormone often associated with a runner's high. Your body's dopamine receptors are located in the brain's frontal cortex, the *same* part of the brain that is headquarters to cognitive reasoning functions. Just as stretching before a workout warms up your muscles to facilitate maximum function, positive affect "warms up" the cerebral frontal cortex, facilitating maximum cognitive function. Who wouldn't want employees who are better problem solvers? The boss who uses the Power of Respect in the workplace is likely to have a workforce with this brainpower advantage, among others.

Nearly half of all workers come back from vacation saying they are not thrilled about going to work.[6] Business leaders need their employees motivated *every* day. With regularity, all of us on the job make assessments about the tasks we have before us. *How challenging are my assignments? How much effort must I exert?* But the biggest assessment is, *Can I accomplish this?* The answer to that question is totally up to you and depends on your *own* assessment of your strengths and competency. Do you think you can? That's where the Power of Respect comes in.

THE POWER OF RESPECT
Being respected enhances your job performance.

It's common sense, really. Being respected enhances your self-image. If someone treats you in a respectful way, you understandably think it's because you *deserve* that respect. When someone makes a point of recognizing you or your contributions, it feels good. You find yourself walking a little taller and permitting yourself to feel just a touch of pride. You *did* make an effort that others recognized as being useful. All of these feelings build upon one another, creating a positive sense of self. As Professor Timothy Judge, now of the University of Florida, puts it, "Positive employees are more motivated to perform their jobs."[7]

Judge has spent years looking at the connection between positivity and job performance. Was there a link, he and his research colleagues wondered, between feeling good at work and doing a good job? The answer is yes. Judge has found that organizations benefit when they put into place policies that foster a positive social and psychological climate, such as giving coworkers help when they need it, making constructive suggestions, and being courteous and respectful to one another.[8]

Considerate Leaders . . .

- Do little things to make it pleasant to be a member of the group.
- Find time to listen.
- Act after consulting members.
- Back up followers.
- Treat members as equals.
- Make others feel at ease when talking with them.
- Put group suggestions into action.

—TIMOTHY A. JUDGE

In one of Judge's studies that looked at the relationship between job satisfaction and a considerate environment, one in which leaders show concern and respect for their followers by looking out for their welfare and expressing appreciation and support for the group, he found that worker job satisfaction and motivation were enhanced.

The group's effectiveness was improved, and workers were generally satisfied with their leader.[9]

Professor Judge tells me that the Power of Respect is something he would consider very much a part of consideration. What makes a considerate or respectful leader? The box on the previous page contains his list. As he says, they are all very respect oriented.[10]

INSPIRE WORKERS TO BE CREATIVE

Tony Hsieh, CEO of Zappos, operates his business by those principles and more. Zappos.com debuted at number twenty-three on the *Fortune* magazine 2009 list of "100 Best Places to Work." It wasn't the online retailer's one billion dollars in gross retail sales that secured the company a place on the list (though that did get them noticed!). It was the fast-growing company's culture that emphasizes collegiality, fun, and respect by giving customer service associates great latitude in doing what they feel is right to satisfy a customer. It must work because 75 percent of Zappos' customers are repeat purchasers.

The Zappos shoe store has grown to include a wide product mix of bags, accessories, clothing, and jewelry. The key to Zappos' phenomenal growth, Hsieh says, is its emphasis on customer service. "We view any expense that enhances the customer experience as a marketing cost because it generates more repeat customers through word of mouth."[11] Zappos offers free shipping on both sales and returns, and while the majority of its business is done online, every page of the Zappos Web site has a toll-free customer service number ensuring a live human is available for help if needed.

Zappos spends very little on marketing, but it is well known for its ease of shopping and depends on word-of-mouth support to get its message out. But the *real* key to Zappos' success is found in its corporate culture, created through core values the employees helped define.

I met Tony Hsieh in the fall of 2008, about the same time the company was going through the first layoffs in its history. Due to the credit crunch, 8 percent of the company's workforce was being let go. It was a challenging time for a firm that is so careful about whom it hires that it offers all potential employees two thousand dollars *not* to take the job after a month-long training program. The thinking is anyone who takes the money is in it for the short haul and not someone who will fit in well with the company culture. The company was just as generous in its layoffs. Each employee was given several months' severance pay as well as six months' paid health coverage.

Zappos' focus on employees is born out of Hsieh's own disappointing experience with an earlier company he cofounded and later sold to Microsoft. LinkExchange was a Web-based ad banner network Hsieh started with a friend. It was hard work in the beginning, but fun. He told me, "When it was five or ten people, we were at our desks all the time. We had no idea what day it was and we would shower just once in a while. Over two and a half years, we hired the people with the right skill set and the right experience, but we didn't know to focus on company culture. By the time it was one hundred people, I didn't want to go to the office anymore. And that's a really weird feeling, because this was a company I had cofounded and I was dreading to go to work."

Determined not to feel that way again, Hsieh invited employees at Zappos to weigh in on what *they* thought the company's core values should be. Hsieh's experience at his old company helped lead to one of those core values being selected.

"One of our core values is to be humble," he explained. "If a computer burner comes in and is supersmart and talented but is egotistical, well, it's really easy not to hire him. At most companies, what they'd say is, 'He's really smart and talented, and yes, he may get on your nerves and is kind of annoying, but he's going to add a lot of value, so let's hire that person.' You keep making compromises like that," he said emphatically, "and that's how a company culture eventually goes downhill."

Setting an example of the company's core value to "be humble," CEO Tony Hsieh takes only a modest salary. (No need to take up a collection; he sold his previous company to Microsoft for over two hundred million dollars!) Hsieh's office is roughly the same size as everyone else's—tiny. It's the company's culture that's really big.

Customers are the lifeblood of any business. The Power of Respect helps businesses solidify customer relationships and protect both the suppliers' and the customers' bottom lines. Challenging times require creative solutions, and the Power of Respect can help inspire workers and leaders to come up with innovative answers to today's challenges.

THE POWER OF RESPECT

The Power of Respect solidifies customer relationships and inspires workers to be innovative.

Whether you're in advertising, manufacturing, product sourcing, or a service-related field, this is a time to recalibrate best practices and reconnect with your customers. Learn about your customers' business and find out how they define success. Can you go beyond the traditional vendor transaction and be a valued partner in anticipating their needs? Have you asked your customers how you could make the relationship better? Asking these questions puts the Power of Respect to work for your business so your customers see interaction with you as a strategic play with benefits far beyond just a commercial transaction.

Zappos Company Core Values

1. Deliver WOW Through Service
2. Embrace and Drive Change
3. Create Fun and a Little Weirdness
4. Be Adventurous, Creative, and Open-Minded
5. Pursue Growth and Learning
6. Build Open and Honest Relationships with Communication
7. Build a Positive Team and Family Spirit
8. Do More with Less
9. Be Passionate and Determined
10. Be Humble[12]

To make sure their company stays focused on their ten core values, prospective employees, or Zapponians as they are called, are first interviewed to make sure they have the skills and technical expertise needed for the position. They then go through a second series of interviews with someone from human resources. It's that second set of interviews that determines if someone is a potential fit at the Web-based retailer.

You might be surprised to hear one of the criteria Zappos looks at during the second round of interviews: "How lucky are you?" Hsieh told me, "At Zappos, that's actually a question on our job application: 'On a scale of 1 to 10, how lucky in life are you?' We generally don't hire the guys who are a 10 because we don't want to bring down our luck." He laughed as he finished, but he cited a research study as the reason behind his company's focus on luck. "The researchers had all the participants go through and count the photos in a newspaper. What the participants didn't know was it was actually a fake newspaper where there were headlines scattered through that said, 'You can stop right now; the answer is thirty-seven, and if you tell the researcher you saw this headline, you get an extra hundred dollars.'"

As Hsieh explained the study, he said that the researchers found the people who consider themselves unlucky in life generally didn't notice the headlines. They just did the task at hand and counted the photos. But most of the people who considered themselves to be lucky noticed the headlines. Hsieh says success is about creating your own luck and being open-minded and always looking for more than what the situation might present itself to be.

> Good luck is another name for tenacity of purpose.
> —RALPH WALDO EMERSON

Zappos' success is dependent on a workforce that is open-minded and motivated as well as empowered to find solutions to their customers' problems. If a customer service representative spends three hours helping one customer resolve an issue, that's fine, as long as the customer is satisfied when he hangs up the phone. A random look at the company's employee blog gives a sense of how workers feel. Entries range from videos of the latest hot

Respectful Bosses . . .

- Treat workers with dignity.
- Give employees a voice.
- Encourage and empower workers.
- Provide feedback and coaching (privately, if appropriate).
- Recognize workers' contributions and achievements.
- Give employees a stake in the company's success.
- Use fair procedures.
- Apologize when they are wrong.

dog social to a shout-out to the "Zapponian of the Day." There's even one excited posting from Tony Hsieh about an order placed from, of all places, McMurdo Station, Antarctica.

Zappos' rapid growth, apparent customer satisfaction, and inclusion on such lists as *Fortune* magazine's "Best Places to Work" and *FastCompany* magazine's "Fast Fifty" would seem to attest that they're doing a lot of things right. But exactly what things?

TREAT YOUR WORKERS WITH RESPECT

The Respectful Bosses checklist contains key points that the body of research on workplace dynamics has determined lead to a sense of workplace respect. That, in turn, leads to workplace stability, which is a hidden savings to any business leader watching costs.

Employees often quit when they feel disrespected. A recent employee survey of more than 370,000 workers by Sirota Survey Intelligence found that workers who feel disrespected are three times more likely to leave their jobs (in a two-year period) than those workers who feel they are treated fairly.[13] Most businesses have their own estimate of the cost of losing an experienced employee. Lost productivity, administrative time spent processing out the departing worker, and interviewing and hiring a replacement, along with training time, all add up. Estimates of the cost are a multiple of an employee's annual salary, so a conservative figure would be one and a half times annual salary. The Labor Department's National Bureau of Labor Statistics puts the annual salary of a professional manager at $97,677, or a total bottom-line cost to the former employer of $146,515. That's $150,000 off the bottom line because an employee didn't feel respected! Another survey estimates two million professionals and managers leave corporate jobs because of workplace bullying and disrespectful comments.[14]

Workers who feel disrespected and unfairly treated don't always just leave their jobs; sometimes they sue the company for wrongful termination. The costs to a business can be astronomical—and a significant portion of them avoidable. In 1975, wrongful termination lawsuits were virtually unheard of. Today America has a litigation mentality that seems to permeate every aspect of business decision making. A 1990 survey by the Bureau of National Affairs of 255 employers found 27 percent of them had been sued for wrongful termination. The average award in those cases was over $600,000, *plus* another $150,000 in legal fees. "We are afraid of being sued by our own employees," said one vice president of a manufacturing company. "It seems to me that if we knew why our own employees would sue us, we could get a better handle on how to avoid lawsuits in the first place."[15]

THE POWER OF RESPECT

The Power of Respect helps businesses minimize costly legal action.

In 1989, General Motors settled a discrimination suit brought by black workers, managers, and professionals. The out-of-pocket costs were estimated to reach forty million dollars. Plaintiffs were able to prove the automaker systematically rated black workers lower for work performed identical to that of whites. It started with a single grievance by a single employee and grew to become a class action lawsuit with more than thirty-eight hundred plaintiffs. General Motors fought the legal action for six years before settling the suit just before the case was set to go to trial.[16]

Duke University professor Allan Lind cites costly legal action as an argument that companies that have what are seen to be as fair procedures are less likely to be the target of litigation. Lind began his research focusing on how people react to their experiences with the law and found over and again that their impressions almost always were linked to whether they thought the process was fair and whether they felt like they were treated with respect. Professor Lind told me, "I didn't start out focusing on respect and fairness, but it just kept coming there."

The day Lind and I spoke, newspaper headlines reflected General Motors' dire financial troubles and the possibility of declaring bankruptcy. I asked about that discrimination lawsuit and wondered out loud if GM had been seen as treating workers with respect, they might not be looking down the road of bankruptcy. Lind responded, "They might not have been. GM and its unions went down this road of 'let's go to the dollars' rather than treating people like people." It's an important reminder at any time, but especially during periods of economic uncertainty.

Ten years after GM's forty-million-dollar lawsuit, the Coca-Cola Company agreed to pay an eye-popping $156 million to settle the largest racial discrimination lawsuit ever. The decade of the 1990s saw an increase of 50 percent of complaints by minorities who felt they'd been discriminated against. Professor Lind says a company's deep pockets are not typically what prompt the legal action. "When I go to explain why someone starts a lawsuit, the inclination is to say, 'Well, they want the money, of course.' But the data suggests it's much more complicated than that. It's often more like, 'Those fellows treated me so disrespectfully, I'll show them.'"

One review of workers found that their perception of fairness in the workplace influenced their contemplation of litigation. Three things were discovered to affect their thinking: the perceived fairness of rules and procedures, the way they were treated at work, and job satisfaction. The authors of the study were

> Do to others what
> you want them to
> do to you.
> —MATTHEW 7:12 NCV

adamant in their findings. "The solution to this dilemma is not in the creation of formal procedures per se, but in the moral and inter-personal conduct of those implementing the procedures."[17] Translated: be nice, be fair, and show a little respect.

The Power of Respect will obviously not find a home in an organization that practices willful discrimination. But it can help minimize costly legal action in companies that do try to operate fairly. Professor Lind writes, "The greatest rule of how to avoid liti-gation should be to treat people fairly, to be considerate and to seek to humanize and dignify the organizational experiences for one's employees and subordinates."[18] This is particularly important at the time an employee is let go. Lind and his team interviewed one thousand people who had been fired or laid off from their jobs in central Ohio.[19] The researchers discovered that the employees' deci-sion to sue was much more heavily influenced by the way they felt they were treated at the time of termination than their view of how they'd been treated during the time of their employment.

> He who does not have the courage to speak up for his rights cannot earn the respect of others.
> —RENÉ G. TORRES

Allan Lind estimates at mini-mum companies save eight thou-sand dollars in legal fees alone for each employee who leaves feeling he or she has been fairly treated when let go. "In the wrongful ter-mination research, what came through clearly is this is a time when people are vulnerable in terms of self-worth and personal identity," he explains. "When that's being removed in a layoff or firing, you are vulnerable and you are looking to see if there is something of me left. Is there something of value left in me? If you are treated with respect, you can say yes, this person treats me as a human being, not as a commodity. If you don't have that, then you have to go into this protective mode, which can be vengeful." More than five million jobs have been lost between December 2007 and April 2009.[20]

GIVE WORKERS A VOICE

Experts on workplace respect say treating employees with dignity, giving them a stake in the company's success and a voice in its affairs, and imparting to them a sense that their contributions are valued and meaningful, result in measurable benefits. In that regard, the medical supply firm PartsSource is a textbook case.

Ray Dalton hasn't had to worry much about wrongful termination lawsuits. His PartsSource Company has an enviable 94 percent employee retention rate. PartsSource is a medical repair parts supplier that did almost one hundred million dollars in sales in 2008. Not bad for a firm that only started in 2001. This fast-paced, fast-growing company hires six to eight new employees each month. It is not for the faint of heart.

"This is a tough place to work," Dalton told me. "It's like a stock market for medical parts. It's fast-paced, it's stressful, and you're on the phone most of the time. Why do we have a 94-percent retention rate? It's because we respect the individual."

It's easy for business leaders to say they respect their employees, and who wouldn't? You sound like a creep if you don't. Visit the PartsSource Web site and one of the first things you see is a testimonial from a customer, lauding the fine work of a PartsSource employee. Also prominently featured are the company's Core Values Statement and its motto: "The Answer Is Yes."[21] Dalton's firm sets an ambitious goal for itself and its employees: to process every medical parts order within an *hour* of the request coming in. To achieve that requires that every worker operate at peak efficiency. There is no room for even one of the two hundred employees to be slackers.

Ray Dalton says the Power of Respect is the foundation of his business. He told me that it starts with the hiring process, but in truth, it starts long before. The secret to PartsSource's success can be found in Compton, California, a rough suburb of Los Angeles where gangs rule the streets and every day is a struggle. Ray Dalton grew up there. While he dropped out of high school, he says the streets of Compton gave him a different kind of education. "You learn to respect other people." Back then, respect was the key to survival for Ray Dalton. Today he says it's critical to his success.

"When you come from humble beginnings, the only thing you can do is come alongside people," he said. Dalton dropped out of high school, joined the Air Force, and then took seven years of night school classes to get his college degree. "I couldn't demand anything because I was bigger. I couldn't demand it because I was smarter than them. I learned the way you get things done is to come alongside people."

Respect is literally part of the job interview at PartsSource. When he's in town, Dalton participates in employee interviews. "I say, 'If you're going to be successful at PartsSource, there are two things you have to understand. One, you will need to find something that you respect about your peers and your leaders, and two, you're going to have to find something they respect about you.'" Ray explained, "When you have respect for someone, all the little things go away. It doesn't matter what color their socks are or what shoes they wear. You have a much higher level of understanding when you respect the value of the person you spend time with."

PartsSource has taken concrete steps to try to foster that culture of respect. Compliments play an important role. Managers are required to compliment someone every day, and it doesn't always come easy. Dalton says it is a learned skill that leaves the giver feeling a bit vulnerable, but the results are worth the initial discomfort. "What do you do when you compliment someone?" he asks. "You show respect. It's just the ultimate gift, to stop and say, 'You did a really good job. I appreciate that.' That moment of respect is a compliment that energizes you to go to the next level. Our feelings are being acknowledged for the efforts we give."

THE POWER OF RESPECT
Businesses with a culture of respect have more satisfied employees.

The Power of Respect is also apparent in the way PartsSource interacts with its customers. The company's philosophy is quite simple: no one calls unless they have a problem, which means they need that problem dealt with promptly and efficiently. That's why PartsSource has no voice mail at the front end. Five full-time telephone receptionists do nothing but answer the phone. "Our tagline is 'The Answer Is Yes!'" says the company's founder. "How can you get a yes answer if you don't get a human being? By having a person answer the call and immediately respond to their question or request, we are telling our customers we respect them."

> ### *Respectful Salespeople . . .*
>
> * Learn about their customer's business.
> * Value the customer's time.
> * Offer solutions.
> * Are polite.
> * Get their facts straight (including names).
> * Speak positively.
> * Seek feedback from their customers.

A hospital in New Jersey found that it suddenly needed to ramp up the telemetry on one of its facilities. Hospital officials called the manufacturer of the equipment, who told them it would be about six weeks to get the site survey completed and probably another six to eight weeks to get the new system installed. This was a *hospital*, where lives were at stake. The folks at PartsSource got a call and within hours they were tracking down antennas and individual components that could be used to cobble together a system that could run off a partial system already in place. In just seven days, the hospital's new system was up and running. Grateful administrators say the "above and beyond" service turned what could have been a three-month project costing $150,000 into a one-week task at a fraction of the cost. Where do you think they'll turn the next time they need equipment?

You'll find that story retold on the PartsSource Web site, along with dozens of other testimonials from happy customers, most of whom name the sales associate who helped meet their needs. Most of PartsSource's customers will never meet their sales associates, since so much business is done via phone and Internet. But Dalton says it's important for the company not to be seen as impersonal. It is one way, he says, of respecting customers.

PartsSource says it tries to respect its workers by giving each of them incentives to make it work. Every person at PartsSource is on some form of variable compensation, even the telephone administrators who get a base salary plus compensation based on how effectively they handle calls. Answer the call before the third ring and it's an extra four to six cents. Transfer the call to the appropriate party and get it answered on the first ring and it's another four to six cents. Having the receptionist motivated to send the call to the right place the first time makes all the difference.

Finally, PartsSource uses the Power of Respect to motivate the executive team. Every spring, the company formulates its strategic business plan for the coming year. Dalton, the CEO, was nowhere to be found as they did. Dalton says the hardest thing he's had to do as an executive is step back and give subordinates a chance to show what they can deliver. "I respected their ability. I put in metrics and measurements so I would be confident they were doing their jobs, and all of a sudden I got balance back in my life. I was excited about doing it again." Dalton says a big part of his job now as CEO is to be Chief Encouragement Officer.

THE POWER OF RESPECT

The Power of Respect can motivate your business team to achieve greater success.

By his own estimate, PartsSource is the tenth company Dalton has founded. He calls himself a "serial entrepreneur" and has been successful enough at it to be named one of Ernst & Young's Entrepreneurs of the Year. Recently, Harvard's Ohio Alumni chapter named him Businessman of the Year, a pretty heady experience for a man with a high school equivalency diploma and a degree from a little-known college. Dalton plays it as a strength. "We are known as the company of second chances," he says. "You look at my 238 employees, and less than 17 percent have any college. A person's worth is not the education he has, but the energy he has to be successful."

Energy is something every business endeavor can use more of, especially when times are tough. Think of the changes in business today. A staggering 5.7 million jobs disappeared between December 2007 and April 2009.[22] Lucky workers who aren't one of the job loss statistics have seen

> Wisdom is worth more than silver; it brings more profit than gold.
> —PROVERBS 3:14 NCV

dramatic changes in their workplaces. They're being asked to handle more tasks, collaborate on more projects, take better care of customers, and come up with ideas to save money. It sounds daunting, but in workplaces where the Power of Respect is present, it is not only doable but likely to be successful.

KEEP YOUR EMPLOYEES INFORMED

Information is critical both to you and your employees. When business prospects look uncertain, it's not easy to forecast the future. Whether you've had layoffs or been able to avoid them, your employees are more concerned about the future than you are. Give them the straight scoop, as much as you can.

Keeping your employees in the loop not only helps them see where the company stands in the big picture but also leaves them with the sense that they are respected, secure in the knowledge that business information is being shared with them because they are important to the overall operation.

People who feel good about themselves are able to handle rapid change well.[23] Being part of a group or team actually helps those positive people perform *better*.[24] Clearly the key is to foster a climate where people feel valued, where they feel a sense of collegiality and common purpose, and where they know where they stand. Goals are clear, work rules are consistent, and support and feedback are constant.

That's not what Anita has at the nonprofit where she works. Read part of her letter to an online support group:

> My CEO makes up policies as she goes. Where policies are in place, she does not adhere to them, so needless to say she ruffles a lot of feathers.
>
> I have seen her humiliate, belittle, bully, and use profanity

when addressing her staff. She micromanages and discriminately gives performance increases, does systemic hiring—the list goes on. She alienates minority staff, so she has no diversity in her corporate office. The turnover rate is astronomical and usually links back to her. If you are not liked by her, she makes your life miserable.

This is a fantastic company with a valuable mission, but the leadership leaves a lot to be desired. The employee morale is so browbeaten that no one is happy or smiles. They're all just working under intimidation and the need for a paycheck. HR has no real role in the company's chain of command. The buck stops at the top, and if you file a grievance, your pink slip is on the way.[25]

Wow! I hope that makes whatever issues you might have at work pale in comparison. If you're reading this book, you probably aren't the kind of boss Anita is struggling with. Her letter makes it easy to see why "presentee-ism" is growing in America: workers show up for their job, do the bare minimum, collect their checks, and head home. Anita may well work for a company with a valuable mission, but it's a safe bet the company is nowhere close to fulfilling its promise. Employees at Anita's firm expect very little from their bosses, and very little is what the bosses get from them.

People perform to their expectations. Psychologists have long known that when all else is equal, people will act in a way that's consistent with their own self-image. Remember Henry Ford's saying, "Whether you think you can or think you can't, you're right"? People whose workplace is imbued with the Power of Respect will tend to "think they can." When people with low self-respect experience failure, their performance drops. But that same failure doesn't seem to slow people with high self-respect. Those with higher self-respect are willing not only to tackle tasks but also to keep at the job until they get it right.[26]

———————————— ❧ ————————————

THE POWER OF RESPECT
People perform to their expectations.

Workers who feel good about themselves and their jobs work longer and harder at their tasks. Since few businesses can afford to have anyone coasting at their jobs, it makes sense to help employees feel good about what they do and where they do it.

Professor Alice Isen, the positive affect expert from Cornell University, has also been exploring the connection between "feeling good" and motivation. Her studies show that workers in a positive frame of mind more readily consider the details of a situation, especially the possible likely outcomes of choices before they choose.[27] Is there a boss or manager around who doesn't want to have employees who consider all the what-ifs before making a move?

People who feel good work longer and for the simple pleasure of the task itself, not in hopes of getting some additional reward. That's called *intrinsic motivation.* They put effort into the task because the task itself is inherently enjoyable. Why do people put together puzzles or play tennis? They simply like doing it. When people are engaged in their work, they get increased satisfaction from it. Often, people who are intrinsically motivated find themselves lost in the flow of the activity.

———————————— ❧ ————————————

THE POWER OF RESPECT
*People who feel good work longer and
for the simple pleasure of the task itself.*

But what about tasks that aren't particularly enjoyable? After all, they do call it "work" for a reason. Isen and her coresearcher,

Johnmarshall Reeve, conducted an experiment in which people in positive affect were given the option of doing an enjoyable task (in this case putting together a three-dimensional cube puzzle enjoyed by the kind of college students involved in the study) or the somewhat tedious task of finding alphabetically ordered letters in pages of random letter sequences (participants would circle "bclpus" but not "cplsyv" or "drpeql"). Isen's studies found that people in positive affect are more strongly influenced by intrinsic motivation—that is, doing a task for the enjoyment. The puzzle problem was enjoyable for the participants. But they did not shirk their "work" responsibilities. When told the letter sequence problem was something important that needed to be done, participants were more likely to work on it than people who were not in a positive frame of mind. Isen concludes that positive affect leads "to forward-looking thinking, self-control, and the ability to stay on task, even on a task that may be uninteresting or unpleasant."[28] Positive affect promotes responsible behavior.

MIRACLE ON 34TH STREET

The ability to sustain effort and count on employees to be responsible is especially critical during times of economic decline and when the task is one with a long time frame. Macy's merger with the May Department Stores Company in 2005 is a good example. The eleven-billion-dollar purchase by Macy's/Federated of the May Department Stores chain created the largest retailer in America. It also created an enormous challenge for CEO Terry Lundgren and his team. Melding different cultures, consolidating regional offices, changing direct reports, integrating information technology systems of merchandising, and even changing the names of stores was a Herculean task fraught with risk at every turn. In cities like Chicago, home to Marshall Field's, some customers expressed outrage over the potential elimination of the venerable store names. Lundgren knew he had his work cut out for him.

Lundgren says one of his first moves as the merger was getting underway was to hit the road and meet face-to-face with local politicians, including the mayors of key cities, such as Chicago, St. Louis, and Boston, as well as May Company executives. First stop: Los Angeles, where the company being acquired had regional headquarters. Since Macy's already had a strong regional presence in San Francisco, it was obvious to everyone that the Los Angeles office would be eliminated.

"We landed at LAX and started driving toward this meeting, and our group was pretty quiet. I wasn't going to lie to anyone. If they had said, 'Are you going to eliminate our division?' I would've said, 'Yeah, unless I learn something here today that changes my mind,'" Lundgren recalled. Along the way, they passed an In-N-Out Burger restaurant, and Lundgren—a Southern California native who calls In-N-Out Burger the "best fast food anywhere"—urged the driver to stop. "I ordered thirty Double-Doubles and a bunch of fries and chocolate and vanilla shakes, and my team and I carried them into this drab Hilton Hotel conference where we were supposed to be having our meeting and a standard luncheon was waiting."

Lundgren said it was totally unplanned. "I walked in, and I said, 'You know you have the best hamburgers I ever tasted right here in LA, and I just had to have one. I hope you're hungry because I brought one for everyone.' They started clapping!" The veteran retailer had a note of wonder in his voice as he recalled the moment. "It immediately broke the ice and when word spread, set a relaxed tone for all our meetings going forward." It may have been a spontaneous moment, but the response was vital for the firm going forward. The Macy's executives had studied the résumés of every May Company manager they were meeting with. They were an extremely talented bunch whose expertise Lundgren considered key to making the merger work. With the exception of those with family relocation conflicts, every single person invited to join the team remained with the newly merged firm.

The Power of Respect can inspire workers to act responsibly and stick with their tasks. But in a company with 165,000 employees, how can any one worker feel important or that the company even knows he exists? Lundgren offers an example of how executives are trying to make it work at Macy's in 2009. As is the case in any merger of similar firms, one of the advantages seen by the brass was the eventual consolidation of various functions—in Macy's case, buying, planning, and marketing—in a unified organization head-quartered in New York. But the retailer didn't want to lose its ability to be responsive to local markets, so the company relocated former buyers and merchandise planners across the country, where they now live and influence the flavor of local stores.

THE POWER OF RESPECT

The Power of Respect can inspire workers
to act responsibly and stick with their tasks.

Local executives are empowered to make what they believe is the right call, and the boss was practically cheering as he described to me how well the process is working. "We've got all this intelligence on the ground," Lundgren gushed enthusiastically, "right where our customers are, and we'd be crazy not to listen to them." Lundgren told me how at the Macy's store in Pittsburgh, the number one sales-man in men's suits asked for Sean Jean suits. Macy's wasn't then selling the Sean Jean brand in that suburban store, but an order for twenty suits was promptly placed based on the sales associate's request. Once the merchandise arrived, the salesman sold sixteen of the twenty suits the first two weeks.

Talk about an employee feeling like he'd been heard! As the store manager told the story, the salesman was totally energized, saying, "Holy cow! I asked for it and you actually got it for me. I guess I'd better sell it!" Lundgren says it brought the request full circle. "The responsibility shifted back to the store to sell it. That's the beauty of this whole thing. The associate listened to his customers and he responded, and we trusted his judgment because he knows his customer best."

That's what respect is all about!

Respect Reminders

───────────── ⁀⁊ ─────────────

- ☐ Encourage employees to share their ideas.
- ☐ Positive workplaces foster better job performance.
- ☐ Workplace respect enhances customer relationships.
- ☐ Disrespected workers are three times more likely to quit.
- ☐ Respectful workplaces have fewer wrongful termination lawsuits.
- ☐ Give compliments at work.
- ☐ Consider your customers' needs.

6

The Leadership Magnet

The Power of Respect for Leaders

2009 was a miserable time to be in the newspaper business. The year opened with some of the nation's most venerable newspapers teetering on the brink. The *Rocky Mountain News* and *Seattle Post-Intelligencer* stopped their printing presses. The *New York Times* came close to shuttering the *Boston Globe,* and there are questions about the financial future of the company itself. The ripple effect of the world's financial crisis put a tourniquet on advertising, which in turn strangled media businesses, both print and broadcast.

So what a surprise it was to schedule a breakfast with the head of the largest magazine publisher in the world and see Ann Moore bound in, full of smiles and optimism. *Doesn't she read the papers?* I found myself wondering as she approached.

"Deborah, how are you? It's been forever." Ann greeted me with a hug. Ann Moore is chairman and CEO of Time Inc., and lately that's been a job that has required a lot of difficult decisions. Moore oversees roughly ten thousand employees around the world who publish more than 115 magazines. 2008 revenues came in at $4.6 billion, off 7 percent from the year before. Our breakfast was scheduled just a few weeks after the company announced that first quarter ad revenues were down 30 percent. Five months earlier, Moore announced a complete reorganization of Time Inc. The company shut down one magazine and announced the layoff of six hundred employees. It has been, as she said in her memo to employees, "a challenge unlike any we've seen before."

Yet Moore is filled with an excitement and anticipation for the future that, frankly, makes you shake your head and wonder what she's taking. It all stems, I learned over breakfast, from her conviction that she's devised the road map to help guide her company through the current economic challenge and help Time Inc. negotiate the paradigm shift that is transforming traditional publishing. You can sum her solution up in one word: *organizing*.

Moore is convinced that the majority of people who work for her—and she suspects this is true across the board in the business world—are overwhelmed by the amount they have to do, frustrated by the paucity of time they have to do it in, and paralyzed by an inability to prioritize. Productivity, customer relations, and creativity are diminished, and all three are vital as the publishing giant repositions itself for the digital future. Moore says we all are suffering from "information overload," and she's made it her mission to do something about it at Time Inc.

The first clues to the problem appeared, she says, in a surprising way. After reorganizing Time Inc. into three divisions and giving pink slips to 6 percent of the workforce, Moore decided she wanted to be sure she and her top managers were on the same page. So she canceled her usual quarterly meeting for the first quarter. She said, "I was tired of standing on stage, and everyone sits in the back, and I am wondering, *Are you really listening to me?* So I decided to have breakfast with our top three hundred executives." Moore says her human resources chief said that was impossible, but the boss prevailed, explaining she could connect with all three hundred if she did breakfasts with fifteen people at a time. "So I did twenty break-fasts in January," she recalls with a laugh.

Moore's intent with the breakfasts was to share in an intimate setting her vision for the company, outline specifics for surviving the downturn, and spell out Time Inc.'s value system. Her objective was to encourage individual executives to get energized and take respon-sibility for their work units. In small groups, Moore and her top lieutenants could talk about their specific challenges, come up with solutions, and speed the pace of change. That is, if everyone came.

Moore says she realized some of her top executives were "so unorganized they couldn't even make it to my breakfast!" With a mix of shock and disbelief in her voice, she told me she overheard her secretary chasing down RSVPs for breakfast with the boss. "She would say, 'You didn't know you had to RSVP? The memo was two sentences!' 'You didn't know it was breakfast? It says in the headline: Breakfast with Ann Moore.' This is information overload. If my top management, my top three hundred people, were not able to sift through the information overload and set priorities, why would I expect anyone else to do the same?"

It sparked a tiny but potentially very meaningful component in the publishing company's recalibration going forward: finding ways to help workers and managers eliminate time wasters that distract them from the job at hand.

Time Inc. took a look at e-mail usage at the firm and found employees were receiving on average twenty thousand e-mails a year! That figures to seventy-five full *days* managing e-mail accounts. Even worse, e-mail traffic was growing at 15 percent annually. Moore says the company set a goal to reclaim fifteen days from the e-mail swamp. Time Inc. now bans e-mails after hours or on weekends, unless it's regarding a breaking news story. Employees have been told to disable the "out of office" auto reply and stop using the "reply all" button, both of which generate e-mails that generally are simply deleted. One survey found Americans spend 2.8 minutes per day deleting e-mail, which calculates to $21.8 billion in lost productivity on an annual basis.[1] Instead of e-mail, folks are encouraged to pick up the phone or speak to a colleague in person. "We have to go back to having more human contact," the Time Inc. executive says.

It seems a small thing for the head of a multibillion-dollar company to focus on. But Ann Moore's success stems from her ability to capitalize on the seemingly insignificant. She says the Power of Respect has been key to her success. "I got the corner office because I figured out how to have respect for women readers," she says. "You can look all over American industry and see people who do not respect their consumers and are not walking in their shoes." She says you have to ask, "How do you make their lives better? How does he or she feel?"

Early in her career at Time Inc., Moore says the company consisted of just five magazines targeting men. "We were dependent on cars, cigarettes, and hard liquor for advertising. It looked pretty shaky to me to have a business built on the cigarette industry, so I said we need a women's magazine around here." Moore moved to the company's then-fledgling *People* magazine, which hit newsstands on Mondays. But as Moore noted, most women do their grocery shopping on Friday. The magazine was stale by then, so delivery was moved to Friday. *People* is now one of Time Inc.'s most profitable magazines. *Real Simple* came out of a single piece of research: the average American woman spends fifty-five minutes a day looking for things. Moore says, "We thought we could solve that problem for her and get her organized."

She's taken that same thought process and turned it on a different group of consumers, the men and women who work at Time Inc. "We've done everything we can," she says. "We've gotten our house in order and lowered our costs; we've invested in and redesigned our products. We've got to wait for General Motors to stabilize and the advertising market to come back, so the best thing

I can do now is invest in the almost ten thousand employees who are here."

At Time Inc., that means back to school. At her series of January breakfasts, Moore asked her top three hundred managers to share the wisdom they've acquired during their careers in publishing with others in the company. Each of the three hundred executives has been asked to design an elective course that employees down the chain of command can sign up to take. Peter Castro, a senior editor at *People* magazine, is teaching the art of the interview. It's not just for reporters. Salespeople who take the class can benefit by learning from a pro the trick to getting people to share information because one of the best ways to make a sale is to learn more about the client and his problems. Martha Nelson, who runs Time Inc.'s entertainment division, teaches a course called "Are You Ready to Be a Boss?" Even CEO Moore has put on her teacher's hat. Her class on team building is specifically aimed at employees with five years or fewer at Time Inc. It's been a real eye-opener for her and her students. "What was shocking to me, Deborah, was that I had some no-shows in my class! I have a waiting list of seventy-five people for these classes. There are only sixteen seats! I mean . . ." Moore was at a loss for words to describe what it was like to see empty chairs in her class.

"How'd that make you feel?" I asked.

"Well, I just . . ." She thought for a moment. "I felt like, what was that all about? You have so little respect for your peers—or *me*?" The CEO's class teaches teamwork, in which the class is asked to play a desert survival game. The only way class members "survive" is if players focus on the group's needs, not their individual ones. "Every semester, I have a dysfunctional team. They have no experience working on a team. I have to open their minds to the idea that I've got to give to you and you've got to take a little from me to be successful. The well-balanced team will always beat the smart individual on average."

The Power of Respect in Leadership

What is it that makes some people good leaders, and what role does the Power of Respect play in transforming leadership from good to great? In his Pulitzer Prize–winning book *Leadership*, James MacGregor Burns first discussed "transformational" leaders who bring organizations forward by inspiring others to "advance to higher levels of morality and motivation." He said, "One of the most universal cravings of our time is a hunger for compelling and creative leadership."[2] Transformational leaders challenge and change perceptions, expectations, and values through their ability to articulate a vision and goals that others will embrace.

THE POWER OF RESPECT
The Power of Respect helps transform leaders from good to great.

A review of leadership research shows that the level of cohesion and degree of personal connection between leaders and followers can make a difference.[3] Leaders who connect with their followers are likely to enjoy greater success. Researchers Bernard Bass and Bruce Avolio defined what qualities make up a transformational leader who can motivate people to higher levels of effort and performance.[4]

- *Idealized influence.* Leaders are admired, respected, and trusted, people whom followers identify with and want to emulate.
- *Inspirational motivation.* Leaders motivate through enthusiasm and optimism, providing work that has meaning and setting appealing future goals.

- *Intellectual stimulation.* Leaders are creative, reframing old problems in creative new ways and questioning old assumptions.
- *Individualized consideration.* Leaders fulfill an individual's need for growth through coaching or mentoring and providing a supportive climate for advancement.

It is easy to see how the Power of Respect is a factor in each of these others-focused leadership styles.

Anyone in a position of leadership—and that pretty much includes all of us at some point during our daily lives—can use the Power of Respect as a tool to inspire the best performance out of our followers.

THE POWER OF RESPECT

The Power of Respect can inspire the best performance from people.

For moms who use the Power of Respect in the family, that means your children will be more likely to clean their rooms and do their homework. For couples, that means your spouse will be less critical. For teachers, that means your students will master the material you're presenting. For business leaders, that means inspiring a stronger work ethic and creative solutions to your company's challenges. The possibilities are endless. Even in international affairs, introducing a tone of respect to tense negotiations can yield positive results.

In July 2008, 56 percent of Americans said the loss of respect for the United States was a "major problem." More than seven in ten Americans told pollsters that they felt the nation was less respected than in the past, an increase from 65 percent just one year earlier.[5] In his inaugural speech, Barack Obama spoke to those concerns, saying, "America is a friend of each nation and every man, woman and child who seeks a future of peace and dignity, and we are ready to lead once more."[6]

"There Is No One Who Doesn't Deserve Respect"

You may not have heard of David Liu, but if you have a friend who's getting married, chances are you'll be using his Web site. David is CEO and cofounder of TheKnot.com, the nation's leading online destination for ideas, inspiration, and resources for anyone planning a wedding. The Web site was born in 1996 out of the frustration David and his wife (and now partner and cofounder), Carley Roney, experienced when trying to plan their own wedding. Today TheKnot .com is a publicly traded company with more than five hundred employees and a network of Web sites aimed at "life stage" consumers: brides, new moms, and new homeowners.

TheKnot.com is one of the Internet's success stories with 3.2 million unique users every month and forty-two hundred new members signing up every day. Yet getting there was a struggle. TheKnot.com launched as a niche site for women at a time when 80 percent of Internet users were men. The company went public in December 1999. The tech bubble burst in April 2000. The company's stock dropped to twenty-six cents. It was a real "hang on by the skin of your teeth" period in the start-up's existence. But TheKnot.com hung on and caught a lucky break with appearances on NBC's *Today*. Since people get married no matter what the economy's doing, the Web site has continued to grow and prosper. The company was relisted on NASDAQ in April 2005. Through this experience, David Liu has learned a lot about leading during challenging times.

"To build a culture is 50 percent of the battle," he told me. "If you have a culture that's hostile and punitive and high pressured, you won't get the best out of people." Liu, a graduate of New York University Film School, learned a lot about how to manage people during his first job after graduation. "I was the admin for a software development company," Liu explained. "I had to answer the phone and make sure the water cooler was filled and fix the copy machine and change the toner. Back then we had floppy drives for the computers. One of my jobs was to format the floppies. It was total grunt work."

Liu was a pathetic gofer. "I was a disaster. I repeatedly accidentally erased the C: drive on the computer," he continued. "My bosses were unbelievably patient and also really nurturing. They probably afforded me a level of respect I didn't deserve. As I look at my own journey, had people not given me a chance and believed in me, I wouldn't be where I am." Those humble moments during Liu's early career shaped his management philosophy. "There is no one too low on the totem pole who doesn't deserve the same respect as anyone else."

David Liu's upbringing also has played a role. "Being the product of an immigrant family, particularly from China, respect was a kind of core value that was embedded in my family. The concept of respecting one's elders or one's teacher is central to Asian culture. There is a certain level of deference that is afforded people who have seniority or positions of knowledge. And if you are an elder, you are supposed to behave in a way that deserves respect."

At TheKnot.com, that plays out in an executive suite that is accessible to the company's five hundred employees. He blogs, contributes to the company intranet, and makes quarterly visits to the firm's locations away from its Manhattan home base. "Much to the consternation of many of the senior executives, I have always had an open-door policy. It's funny. When you start off with seven people working 24/7, it's not that controversial," Liu told me. "Anyone should feel comfortable coming into my office and expressing themselves about anything. To me, that's a check and balance. If management knows that you will sit and talk to their report, they will exercise better judgment." Liu also said his open-door policy keeps him from being relegated to the "ivory tower."

Leadership research confirms that openness, as found at TheKnot .com, can be an important tool in employee motivation. When people are allowed to present suggestions or participate in the resolution of problems or conflicts, they feel they are more fairly treated. People whose views are heard judge the process as fair and react more positively to the outcome.[7] When people see their input as being meaningful, they reciprocate by investing more time and energy in their jobs. Employees whose bosses give them a say also see their leaders as more trustworthy, "i.e., the authority listens to me and uses this information to make the best possible decision."[8] In this context, trust "refers to the extent to which people think that the authority is concerned about others' well-being and will act in ways that serve the interests of these others."[9]

THE POWER OF RESPECT

People who feel respected will invest more time and energy in their jobs.

THE BENEFITS OF BEING HEARD

New York University psychology professor Tom Tyler found that friction within organizations and relationships can be minimized simply by giving people a voice in the situation.[10] "More than any other issue," he writes, "treatment with dignity and respect is something that authorities can give to everyone with whom they deal." Tyler says the importance that people place upon politeness and respect is especially relevant to conflict resolution. Employees sense that if their opinions are at least heard, the bosses value and will protect their interests.[11] Giving employees a say in what's happening boomerangs back in that it encourages the employee to be more cooperative with the objectives of the employer.[12]

At TheKnot.com, employees learned their bosses were paying attention to their suggestions when a new executive on a listening tour to various departments detected friction between the ad operations and ad sales groups. As David Liu described the conflict, "Each side thought the other was messing up, and there was concern that we were losing vendors because of internal procedures. They came up with a process where everyone was incentivized by renewals." Liu said the employees suggested they be cross-trained, each unit instructed to the other's processes so they could speak on each other's behalf.

It was a monumentally brilliant suggestion—one that came from the operations people directly. "It completely changed the tenor of the groups. They are more collaborative and focused." Liu told me that it inspired others

> Boldness has genius, power, and magic in it.
> —GOETHE

in the company to take on more responsibilities. "All of a sudden our customer service people said they wanted to be trained on how to upsell. 'Did you know we could actually do this too?'" Liu recalled that they asked. The end result for the Internet company is a wider circle of energized employees, each of them *looking* for ways they can make a positive difference to the company and its bottom line. A pretty impressive return for something that cost absolutely nothing—but time.

⟨❦⟩

THE POWER OF RESPECT

*Leaders who use the Power of Respect have
more satisfied, productive workers.*

Inspirational leaders are not only energetic and optimistic, but they also use the Power of Respect to tap into their followers' needs for work that is meaningful, for work where they can make progress, and for jobs where they are treated decently.

Any employer will tell you that the jobs their workers do are meaningful, that progress happens every day or the business would go under. But how many *workers* are told their efforts make a difference? Leaders who use the Power of Respect to support their employees and let them know their hard work is valued have employees who not only feel good about working there, but the quality of their work is also enhanced.

Five Properties of a Good Organization

1. Purpose—Shared vision of its goals reinforced by remembrances and celebrations
2. Safety—Protection against threat, exploitation, and danger
3. Fairness—Equitable rules regarding rewards and punishment and how these should be meted out
4. Humanity—Display of mutual care and concern
5. Dignity—Treated respectfully as individuals within the organization, regardless of their position[13]

Take a closer look at the specifics of how the CEO of Time Inc. handled the challenge of refocusing the company during a period of tremendous pressure. After the reorganization, her first step was to listen to her top lieutenants. The usual management presentation event that finds executives talking at staff rather than with them was eliminated, replaced by manageable, small meetings where real specifics and practical solutions were discussed. A key annoyance for some, a problem for others, excessive e-mail was targeted and steps taken to bring it under control. The Time Inc. University gave up-and-comers the opportunity to learn more about areas where their careers could advance, often in the company of some of the most important players in the firm.

Organizational leadership experts would say it is a textbook example of providing employees with "voice," a chance to be heard; "consideration," the knowledge that management has acted on a frustration of many employees (that unruly e-mail); and the possibility of "advancement," something important in fostering employee loyalty.

THREE THINGS THAT MOTIVATE PEOPLE

Anyone hoping to use the Power of Respect as a leadership tool needs to understand what motivates people.

Significance

Sociologists tell us that one of man's strongest urges is to matter. People want to feel valued, to have a sense of purpose. We want to know that our contributions make a difference. My own sense has long been that the final question we will ask ourselves is, *Did I matter? Was my existence on this planet for a purpose?*

Community

People also want to belong. We crave association with others, so rather than risk relationships, we generally overlook small infractions. We participate in groups and perceive our rank in those groups as a gauge to determine our status. People are dependent on our fellow humans for physical survival. Our performance in almost everything is enhanced when we are in the company of people about whom we feel positive.

Zest

People are motivated by that extra edge, the electricity that comes when one knows they're part of something special. It's the pleasure that comes from creative pursuits. It's the contentment that comes from seeing work as a calling and from being happy with life in general.

Respect helps communicate information relative to these three states, all of it relevant to one's identity. Being respected confers acceptance and status. Students and employees alike often find themselves being asked to work in groups. Relationships are more important than ever in business. In order to be effective, your opinions must be valued and welcomed by clients or fellow group members. The key to all of these is respect.

THE POWER OF RESPECT

In order to be effective, you have to earn people's respect.

WHAT EMPLOYEES ARE REALLY THINKING

Harvard University Business School professor Teresa Amabile has spent twenty-six years researching organizations and says that productivity and creativity are strongly related. She says leaders' behavior can make a huge difference in fostering both. Amabile and her coresearcher Steven Kramer got a rare look at what really goes on in people's minds when they are at work. For five months, they received daily diaries from 238 professionals working on creative projects at seven different companies. By the end, they'd collected nearly twelve thousand daily reports describing an event that stood out that workday in the employees' minds, how they felt about it and how it made them feel. The entire team participated in submitting these confidential daily e-mails, so the researchers had a complete picture of what was going on at the companies.[14]

What was immediately apparent was how much workers think about what goes on at the job. They're trying to make sense of events and making conclusions about what they're being asked to do, which in turn affects their level of motivation for their work.

For example, if your boss is slow to respond to your request for a meeting, the thought process that results could go something like this: *I asked my boss for a meeting a week ago. I need to show him where we stand on that project he tasked me with. He's not interested in what I am doing. This project must not be that important to the business. They're assigning me unimportant busywork, so I must not be very valuable here. Oh no—my job may be in jeopardy! I haven't looked for work in ten years, and the economy stinks right now. I haven't put enough in an emergency fund, and I've got one kid in college and another headed there next year. What am I gonna do?*

Because the boss was not prompt in responding to an employee, the employee now wonders if he may soon be unemployed. It's the thought process of an alarmist, to be sure, but also an understandable one. The lack of communication—on both sides—has left one individual gravely concerned about his job and the other in the position of perhaps having to soon find and train a new worker. The employee, who is thinking about and processing what is going on at his job, now feels disrespected and unimportant.

And that notion of performing well under pressure? It's usually wrong, according to Professor Amabile's research. "When people are 'on a treadmill,' running from one unrelated task to another, 'fighting fires,' they are unable to focus on any single problem for very long," she says. "The creativity of their work is lower." When time pressures cannot be avoided, the negative impact can be mitigated if a boss makes sure that workers understand why the task is urgently important for the team or the organization or the clients—and if the boss does what he can to protect the employees from unrelated distractions or interruptions. When employees focus on "a mission" like this, time pressure can stimulate their creativity.[15]

Similarly, employees who have negative feedback toward company decisions resist the changes when they don't feel that their opinions are heard or valued. When one company announced an acquisition, the reaction among some workers who were keeping diaries was the decision was "boneheaded" and "people are walking around scared and afraid for their jobs."

> So much of what we call management consists of making it difficult for people to do work.
> —PETER DRUCKER

Yet consider the difference in employee morale when the Power of Respect was implemented in such a situation. When a critical project required workers to work fifteen-hour days, the diary entries from employees in Amabile's research study read, "I have been here about fifteen hours, but it has been one of the best days I've had in months," and "People are working crazy hours . . . Wonderful Miss Ellen [the project manager] is doing a great job keeping us going." These diary entries were written the same day company bigwigs visited to express their appreciation for the extraordinary effort, bringing pizza and bottled water to the job site.

Sometimes one of the best things a leader can do is get out of the way. Professor Amabile told me, "The most important thing is to facilitate progress itself on meaningful work while giving people empowerment. That means paying attention to the ordinary needs that people have and the ordinary obstacles people might be encountering and doing something about them day by day." That means checking in and keeping tabs on workers, but not hovering. If a worker designing a computer program is stymied because he doesn't know the precise metrics the client will need, the boss who checks in will be able to hound the client to get the information, facilitating the worker's progress. Amabile says facilitating also means "helping people step back and see the progress they have made, despite inevitable setbacks, and using the setbacks as learning opportunities to move forward." The biggest boost to workers is to know they've done good work and it's been recognized.

The residual effects of this are huge. Those same workers who have experienced the Power of Respect and feel good about themselves and the job they do will persist longer in the face of failure.[16] Employees who think positively of themselves and their work are also more effective in team contexts, and teams are increasingly important in business today.[17]

RESPECT GENERATES CREATIVITY

Employees who feel respected at work also come up with better ideas. People are much more creative when they are positively motivated, and you might be surprised by what the best motivation is. It isn't money. A look at the output of more than eleven thousand research and development workers in service and manufacturing companies found those who were "intrinsically" motivated—that is, motivated by the intellectual challenge of the job they were given—were more productive, especially during the early phases of the work.[18] Independence was also shown to be a positive motivator. Workers who were assigned a task and given the tools and authority to go ahead and complete it were also motivated. Of course, salary was important, but extrinsic factors (such as salary, benefits, and job security) were not as strong drivers of creative output as intellectual challenge.

In one survey, 40 percent of workers said they would leave their current jobs for another if it offered greater challenges and career development. Money was not the motivator. Ironically, the accounting firm Deloitte found that 70 percent of the employees who left for new positions could have found those same jobs and careers within the company.[19] People stay in a job when they see it has a future. Employers benefit when they do.

Professor Amabile told me that in her study, people were more than 50 percent more likely to have creative ideas when they saw what was going on at work in a positive light. Those were the times employees felt they'd had good days at work. In one participant's daily diaries, she listed twenty episodes of creative thinking. Eighty percent of that creative thinking came after days in which her mood was higher than usual. This means business leaders can use the Power of Respect to enhance their workers' creativity and productivity by providing focus for the task and independence to accomplish it, appreciation for accomplishment and effort, and regular feedback.

THE POWER OF RESPECT

*Leaders can show respect to their team
by getting out of the way.*

A TEAM APPROACH

At Macy's, CEO Terry Lundgren has staked the retail giant's future on the team approach. He says when company executives recognized the economy was headed south and likely to stay there, they gathered the firm's best thinkers together in late 2008 to strategize. "We said, 'If you were starting a new company today, a twenty-five-billion-dollar retailer, what would it look like?'" Lundgren recalled. "'How would you organize yourself, and who would be the leaders? Because if ever there is a time to reinvent yourself, 2009 is the perfect time to do it.'" The result was a strategy called "My Macy's," sixty-nine local districts that will oversee small groups of stores on a micro basis. Buying, planning, and marketing are all centrally located, but these smaller units around the country are managed by team members, many of whom are former buyers and merchandisers. They are charged with drawing from the overall vision that will be set centrally and tweaking it to make it relevant for customers who shop at each location.

The reorganization at Macy's, necessitated in part by the downturn of the economy, is a perfect example of the kind of intellectual stimulation researchers say is part of respectful leadership. They are reframing old problems in new ways and engaging workers to help come up with solutions.

The innovation and creativity that comes when the Power of Respect is demonstrated in the workplace by engaging employees in the company process can be the difference between survival and death in the marketplace. The photographic film business is a perfect example. Critics of Eastman Kodak say the iconic filmmaker focused for too long on enhancing its chemical-based film products and was late to the game of digital imaging. Contrast that to Fujifilm. The Japanese maker of film created a centralized R&D lab during a restructuring in 2006 and found new applications for processes it had developed in the analog film business. Digital imaging was a no-brainer move, but Fujifilm also moved into the flat-panel display business, manufacturing a protective coating using the same chemical that used to coat analog film. Fuji president Shigetaka Komori also held countless meetings with small groups throughout the company and asked the top one thousand employees to send him a two-page memo suggesting opportunities and challenges they saw from

> To lead the people,
> walk behind them.
> —LAO-TZU

their perspective. There are often brilliant business ideas to be found throughout an organization. Smart leaders find ways to empower their subordinates to share them.

INSPIRATIONAL LEADERS "WALK THE WALK"

There is perhaps no more vibrant way for leaders to employ the Power of Respect than for followers to see them "walk the walk." What is the leader doing that makes him or her seem relatable?

As mentioned in chapter 5, University of Florida professor Timothy Judge has spent years exploring the connection between consideration and effective leadership. His review of the academic literature published on the subject found consideration is a "fundamental indicator of effective leadership."[20] Consideration is the degree to which a leader shows concern and respect for members of a group. His team discovered that consideration was strongly related both to follower satisfaction and motivation as well as leader effectiveness. The ways of doing this are endless.

It could be as simple as being accessible. When Robert Ingram was CEO of the pharmaceutical giant Glaxo, he made it a point each month to visit one of the company's plants and have breakfast with everyone whose birthday fell within that month. There was no agenda beyond giving employees an opportunity to talk about what was on their minds. Eventually everyone knew someone who'd eaten breakfast with the boss.

THE POWER OF RESPECT
Respect people by being accessible.

When he was building Citigroup into the world's largest financial institution, former CEO Sandy Weill says he "did a lot of management by walking around." Now involved in actively managing his philanthropic interests, Weill met with me in his Fifth Avenue office, where the view out the windows is a spectacular Manhattan skyline, and a glance toward the walls reveals a lifetime of memories of the famous and infamous with whom he has crossed paths.

"You can learn a lot by speaking to people down in the ranks," Weill told me. "You get a better feel of what is going on in the company. How people react to things." Weill recalled that during the days of Citigroup's rapid growth, it was doubly meaningful to have the CEO unexpectedly show up. "Years ago, the computers used to break down. I spent many a night sleeping in the computer room. Not that I knew anything about how to fix it," he laughed. Somehow I just couldn't picture Mr. Weill cuddled up on the computer room floor. He continued, "But I was there just to keep the guy trying to fix it company. Trying to let him know that we think that what he does has an important function."

At many companies, leaders can be seen as "one of us" if they share in the financial pain being felt elsewhere in the organization. Not yet gone, but on the wane, are days of first-class airfare, executive dining rooms, and compensation packages for executives in the CEO suite. John Thain may have reimbursed Merrill Lynch the cost of his $1.2 million redecorating job, but the damage was already done. At a time when the company's very existence was in the balance, the purchase of such things as an eighty-seven-thousand-dollar rug and fourteen-hundred-dollar wastebasket made Mr. Thain appear out of touch with and aloof from the rest of the banking firm's employees.

TheKnot.com's David Liu turned down a pay package offered him by his board during the third quarter of 2008. "I didn't think it was appropriate given the economy. I turned down the higher salary and the bonus. It's not well known, so I don't get the 'goodwill credit,' but it does set a different tone to get people to be more responsible."

Over at Macy's, Lundgren and the rest of the executive team led the charge to eliminate one of the most coveted perks at the company: the executive merchandise discount. Far more generous than the standard employee discount, the retailer's top one thousand employees, all of them senior executives, got the extra discount. Lundgren told me the rationale behind it was, "'We have to wear new suits and new dresses all the time in meetings with designers and heads of companies.' Well, I eliminated the discount—and it was a good one! Now we get the same discount as a sales associate or the manager of the store in Queens." Lundgren says the team tried to eliminate or reduce most executive benefits as part of a relentless search for expense reductions. But the discount *was* a controversial subject. At a time when the economy is so challenging and executives more than fairly compensated, Lundgren said it was the right thing to do.

> Loyalty means nothing unless it has at its heart the absolute principle of self-sacrifice.
> —WOODROW T. WILSON

It's also the smart thing to do. People are inspired by the self-sacrifice of others. The entire world was dumbfounded by the selfless act of Captain Richard Phillips in giving himself over to pirates off the Somali coast in exchange for the safety of his crew. The daring rescue by members of the Navy SEAL unit only added to the remarkable tale. That the Navy marksman was able to take out the pirates without harming the hostage sea captain left everyone speechless.

Americans were similarly awed by the bravery under unspeakable pressure exhibited by Captain C. B. "Sully" Sullenberger when US Air flight 1549 was landed in the Hudson River. The only casualties were the geese that caused both engines of the Airbus 320 to fail. Even as the plane was sinking into the waters of the Hudson, Sullenberger would not exit the plane until he had walked through the plane—twice—to make sure all 155 passengers and crew were safe.

Researchers say self-sacrificial acts like these are one of the most direct ways for leaders to communicate that the group's welfare is important to them.[21] Leaders who share in the burdens of the job as well as the rewards have a positive impact on their followers. They are generally more effective and seen by followers as charismatic. Charismatic leaders are said to be better able to get followers to embrace their vision for the future. They inspire higher levels of performance and deeper levels of commitment and satisfaction among workers.[22] When people see others do the right thing, it rubs off.

Respect Reminders

- ☐ Win cooperation by letting followers have a say.
- ☐ Treat everyone with respect.
- ☐ Assure employees that their tasks are meaningful.
- ☐ Provide independence and constructive feedback.
- ☐ Recognize good work—publicly.
- ☐ Be seen as a leader who personally sacrifices for the good of all.

7

It's on the Inside

The Power of Self-Respect

J.R. Martinez has always been the kind of guy who gets noticed. In high school, he was the good-looking kid on the football team with the dazzling smile. Happy-go-lucky and eager to please, J.R. was known and liked by everyone at Dalton High School. J.R.'s plan was to get recruited for college football and one day play for the NFL, but he'd taken too many technical classes in high school and wasn't eligible for Division I colleges. Plan B was the U.S. Army.

On April 3, 2003, J.R. was driving a Humvee near Karbala, Iraq, one of the last vehicles in a nearly one-hundred-unit-long convoy. It was midway through his fourth week in Iraq. J.R.'s mates in the truck were joking about "how cool it would be to earn a Purple Heart." Moments later, Martinez's truck hit a land mine. The Hummer burst into a fiery ball. The light was blinding, the heat excruciating. The other three soldiers in the vehicle escaped with minor injuries. J.R. was trapped, belted in, screaming for anyone to help him.

Two images flashed though his mind. The first was his mother, standing in a cemetery being handed a folded American flag. The second was a face he had not seen since he was five years old. It was that of his sister, Anabelita, who had died. J.R. says his sister told him, "You can't go because Mom needs you."

The next thing Martinez remembers is waking up on the side of the road in absolute agony. He was being cradled by his sergeant who rocked him, telling J.R. he'd be okay. J.R. told me he would try to touch his face, and his sergeant held his arms back. His wounds were massive. Virtually the entire left side of J.R.'s body was burned, his skin literally melted away. The only part of his left arm that was unscathed was the strip of skin beneath his watchband. His ears and nose were practically gone. J.R. was burned over 40 percent of his body. Martinez was evacuated to Landstuhl Medical Center in Germany and from there to the burn unit at Brook Army Medical Center in San Antonio, Texas. His recovery lasted thirty-four months. He has endured thirty-two operations.

J.R. tells me his darkest day was the moment he looked in the mirror. The handsome young man for whom all the girls swooned did not stare back. Instead, the reflected image the young army man saw made him recoil. For a time J.R. contemplated suicide. J.R.'s mother knew what was wrong. "She said, 'It's the girls. You're afraid no girl will ever want you,'" J.R. told me. "She was right. I thought, *How is society going to accept me like this? How are the people going to look at me? I'm nineteen years old. I don't want to live like this; there is no hope.*"

Martinez says for him the war didn't really begin until he left the burn unit and returned to his hometown. "When I came, the real war started," he says. "I was really nervous about coming back. How would everybody react to me? Would they even know who I was?" The reception J.R. got from his hometown left him speechless. Everyone, it seemed, turned out to cheer his return. His former high school gym was filled to the rafters for a pep rally. It was a turning point for the wounded soldier.

"I realized then what truly matters is who you are on the inside.

The people in Dalton, Georgia, loved me for who I was, not my appearance or what I was going to look like in the future. It was for who J.R. was." J.R. spoke to the kids at his old high school, some of whom had been students when he was there. He talked about sacrifice. He talked about challenges. He talked about finding a purpose. The kids were spellbound. J.R. knew then what his next mission would be.

J.R. says it was the constant presence of his mother by his bedside that helped him move forward. That, and that image of his late sister. "I really feel that my sister lives on through me. That I have important work to do," J.R. says.

> Be beautiful if you can, wise if you want to, but be respected. That is essential.
> —ANNA GOULD

That work, J.R. believes, is to serve as an advocate for people who've met with adversity, especially wounded soldiers. "I have scars on the outside, where they are visible. But there are thousands of people who have them inside where nobody even has a clue. They are the ones who are dealing with trauma and not always getting the help they need." J.R. says in a lot of ways, he has it easier than the men and women who don't bear physical scars. People see his scars and know he's an Iraq war veteran. They are immediately sympathetic and supportive. J.R. speaks forcefully about the need for the nation to do more to help those vets with psychological wounds.

Today, J.R. Martinez is an advocate for various veterans and wounded servicemen's groups. He travels the nation as a motivational speaker. And he even discovered a new career that might strike you as amazing.

Actually, when you know J.R. Martinez, it really isn't so surprising. What J.R. Martinez has come to realize since his injury is it wasn't his "pretty boy" looks that made him such a popular kid during his high school days. It was his winning smile and his exuberant personality. There isn't a fire big enough to remove that. The more J.R. has talked about his experiences, the more confident he has become in himself. He says, "Despite what you may go through in life, you never quit. You have hope and you have patience and you dream, because if you can do those things, you can accomplish anything in life."

That Power of Self-Respect brought J.R. Martinez to the set of *All My Children*. I cannot begin to describe the utter delight in J.R.'s voice when he called me at the end of the summer of 2008 with the incredible news. "Deb, guess what! You're never going to believe!" J.R. said excitedly. "I'm going to be on *All My Children*." He was right, I didn't believe it. When he finally convinced me he wasn't joking, I figured he was making a quick one-shot appearance on the soap opera, and maybe we'd have time to have dinner while he was in New York. Wrong. J.R. has a recurring role on the show.

Always plugged in, J.R. had heard that ABC had put out a casting call for a real war veteran to play the part of a wounded soldier. Out of six hundred people who auditioned, J.R. Martinez got the part—practically the moment he read the script. Of course I had to tell this story on *Inside Edition*. When I interviewed *All My Children* casting director Judy Blye Wilson, she told me J.R.'s "spark" and zest for life made him stand out. He got the part two weeks after his screen test.

The story line calls for J.R. to play the part of an army lieutenant wounded in the Iraq war. His fiancée thinks he is dead—and given the severity of his injuries, J.R.'s character lets her keep thinking that. The suspense in the story is whether he will ever come face-to-face with his love and let her see him for what he is.

In real life, J.R. Martinez got over that a long time ago. He's making a difference in the lives of others as a result. He knows this because of the e-mails he has gotten from his fans. There was the guy who wrote of his own challenges, "I'm going to step up to the plate

right now. I'm going to deal with it. I'm going to move forward."
There was the young woman who shared with him, "I myself have
wondered at times what God has planned for me, and through many
years I've come to accept that I'm a giver also and through your gifts
and huge heart I see a great future in store for you. Oh yes, and as
far as that 'pretty boy' comment, you have surpassed that all the way
to gorgeous. That smile is intoxicating . . . embrace it!" Someone
else thanked J.R. for his service, adding, "You have inspired me to
look at my own life a little closer."

J.R. has inspired me to look at my life a little closer too. Would
I have been able to handle with such grace the challenges he has
endured? J.R.'s studio is just a couple of blocks away from where we
shoot *Inside Edition* every day. Sometimes when I see J.R., I study
his face. The scars that seemed so pronounced when I first met this
extraordinary young man seem to have faded. That's because the
accident that caused them does
not define who J.R. Martinez is.
J.R.'s blazing smile, his sparkling
eyes—that's what you notice
about J.R. Martinez. I keep telling him, "J.R., one day you are
going to meet a very lucky girl."
But he's in no rush to do that
just now. J.R.'s got a lot of important work to do, and there are
plenty of people who benefit from hearing his story. It really is a
story of the Power of Self-Respect.

> Self-respect is the
> cornerstone of all
> virtue.
> —JOHN HERSCHEL

THE LIBERATING POWER OF SELF-RESPECT

J.R. Martinez's sense of self-respect was restored after his injury
because he recognized the value of his life was not connected to the
visual appearance one presents to the world. The war in Iraq ended

for J.R. when he embraced the inner man with the changed exterior. He no longer worried or cared what strangers might think.

Obviously everyone cares about how others see them. But how much of your sense of self is impacted by what *someone else* does or says in relation to you? The answer depends in part on who that someone is. You may not like your boss, but your future at work depends on having a good relationship, so a slight from him or her is meaningful. A callous comment from your spouse, the person you live with, definitely leaves a mark. But being ignored by your brother-in-law at a family wedding? Who cares? You probably won't see him until the next family event, if then. It's that huge group of people in the middle who have the potential to sting us with their disrespectful comments and inconsiderate acts.

Think for a moment. Is that really *self*-respect? If you let others' opinions determine how you feel about yourself, aren't you actually giving *others* the power to dictate how you feel about you? Why would you do that?

What *is* it that you respect about yourself? Don't you wish you could do a sort of full body scan to decide what qualities about you that you admire? Instead of an MRI, let's call it an SRI—a Self-Respect Inspection.

SELF-RESPECT INSPECTION

A self-respect inspection is not unlike the annual checkup the motor vehicle department requires you make of your car. Like your motor vehicle inspection, it's a two-pronged process. One checkup details the qualities that ideally your car will have (inflated tires, windshield free from cracks, functioning turn lights) while the other checkup is brutally honest about the present state of affairs (the bumper is missing, your headlight is smashed, the passenger side is missing a seat belt).

On an SRI, you first articulate what qualities you would ideally like to possess and then assess which ones you already have. You may balk at the thought of doing this, but this is not an "I wish I were fifteen pounds lighter" exercise. It is an opportunity to list traits you find admirable or essential in a quality person, then assess how many of or to what degree you have those traits. Take a moment to list what you consider to be admirable traits in the following areas:

SRI Step One:
Respectable Traits

- **Work Ethic**—focused, dedicated, earnest, reliable, energetic, creative
- **Treatment of Others**—thoughtful, inclusive, proactive, self-sacrificing
- **Personal Growth**—read, explore, experiment, challenge old perceptions
- **Philanthropy**—give time or money, involved in issues bigger than self, participate in a cause
- **Patience**—considerate, humble, deliberative

As you go through this exercise, you may find yourself stumped trying to think of qualities to consider. You know a virtue when you see it, but if you can't see it, how can you consider it? The Values in Action—Strengths in Character assessment done by Professor Martin Seligman of the University of Pennsylvania and Professor Christopher Peterson of the University of Michigan provides a gold mine of thought-starter material. The psychologists assembled the list in an effort to quantify the attributes of happy, satisfied people. The list, which includes such traits as creativity, kindness, wisdom, honesty, and gratitude among others, are attributes that Peterson and Seligman's research indicates contribute greatly to a person's sense of fulfillment and character. You can find the complete list of character strengths in the appendix of this book.

Having taken note of what kind of work ethic, approach to dealing with others, value system, and so on that *you* find admirable, ask yourself, *How do I stack up? What qualities about myself do I admire? What virtues guide my choices? Am I a person of convictions who doesn't back down in the face of challenge? What is it about me that is worthy of respect?*

This list is not about tangible things, like promotions or awards. It's about intangibles. What is your capacity for hard work? What are your beliefs about compassion? Are you the sort of person who tries to find the silver lining in every circumstance? How is that an asset? Look for meaningful traits that, were they used to describe someone else, you'd want to emulate.

Deborah's SRI

- **Capacity for hard work**—I'm not afraid or too proud to take on mentally or physically difficult or time-consuming tasks.
- **Loyal**—I don't forget my friends, but I am sad when they forget me.
- **Curious**—I love to find out new things and actually *enjoy* doing research.
- **Giving**—I try to make a difference in the world. (This book is an example.)
- **Thoughtful**—I don't do things rashly.

As you go through this process, you will inevitably come up with plenty of things you don't find appealing about yourself. You might want to jot those on a separate sheet of paper to deal with later. Right now, the goal is to focus on what aspects of yourself are to be admired, emulated, praised. While the emphasis is not on your particular abilities, you may want to note that you are a gifted pianist. Your skill may indeed be part God-given talent, but it was inevitably hours and hours of tedious practice that helped you become the spectacular musician you are. That tenacity and dedication of purpose would certainly make your list of admirable traits.

My own Self-Respect Inventory is on the opposite page. I debated whether to share it, but I figured if I'm teaching you this technique, I ought to show you that I try to practice this in my own life. As I look at my list, I can't help but laugh and notice that a faithful bloodhound and I have a lot in common! As I made that list, I was also coming up with plenty of areas that I need to work on. I could stand to be more spontaneous. A little spur-of-the-moment frivolity wouldn't hurt. Nowhere in there does it say I take good care of myself physically; the treadmill and I have an uneasy relationship. It sits there and reminds me by its presence that I should get on the thing. I stare back and regret ever buying it in the first place. Like everyone, I have plenty of work to do in other areas of my life.

Take a moment to focus on your positive attributes and create your own personal Self-Respect Inventory.

Your SRI Report

Quality   Ranking (1–7)

_____   _____

_____   _____

_____   _____

_____   _____

Scores of 3 and above mean your self-respect
is headed in the right direction!

Review your SRI and look at your list of good qualities. If someone else had those traits, you'd admire and respect those qualities, no questions asked. Why withhold the credit these virtues are due simply because they are your virtues? Spend time contemplating your list. Self-respect is strengthened when you realize your values hold up under scrutiny. Remind yourself that these are worthy qualities. They are to be admired in an individual. You are to be commended because these are value strengths you possess. Give yourself between one and seven points based on how strongly you believe you are embracing these qualities.

What you have created is a realistic snapshot of your finer points. If you are feeling bold, you might share your SRI report with a loved one or close friend. They likely have some additional positive qualities to add to the list.

***

THE POWER OF RESPECT
Respect plays a huge role in how we feel about ourselves.

That SRI you just took should have provided you with valuable information to help solidify your sense of self-respect. Why is it such an important exercise? Because a strong sense of self-respect can act as a protective barrier against perceived and real slights. Self-respect is the product of two things: what you think of yourself and what you believe others' opinions of you are. Psychologists have determined that the way we think we are being treated influences our sense of self-worth.[1] When we are treated fairly, with dignity and respect, it positively impacts our self-evaluation and sense of acceptance.[2] Feeling respected promotes self-confidence and a sense of identity.

While the respect we have for ourselves plays a huge role in our self-image, the degree to which we feel we have been treated respectfully also impacts how worthy and important we feel.[3] When people feel respected, they more readily cooperate in an effort for the public good.[4] When an authority figure treats members of a group respectfully, group members are more committed to the organization.[5]

When group members identify with the values of the organization, they do the right thing. As Zappos.com CEO Tony Hsieh mentioned earlier, the online retailer has a ten-point list of the company's core values. Number ten is "Be humble." It starts at the top. Hsieh's quiet manner and casual clothes give no hint of his rank. Thanks to its rigorous screening process, the company only hires people it feels have the "right ethical stuff" to work there. Hsieh likes to tell the following story to prove it. A customer had purchased a wallet, tried it out, and then returned it later for a refund. The minimum-wage clerk who was processing the return opened the wallet and found $150 cash inside. There isn't a lot of security in the Zappos warehouse. The clerk could have probably kept the money, and no one would have ever known. The customer never imagined she'd left the cash in the wallet; she thought her children had taken it. She was stunned when the money was returned to her along with a personal note from the clerk, who I am willing to bet just couldn't have slept at night if he'd kept the money. The Power of Self-Respect is fostered by a supportive workplace.

People who feel good about themselves are more honest. They treat others well, they are sensitive to the needs of others, and they tend to be positive. People who feel a strong sense of self are more likely to be achievers because they're willing to take risks to achieve their dreams.

> If I respect myself, it does not trouble me if others hold me lightly.
>
> —MAX NORDAU

People with a more positive self-image are likely to be less dependent on respect for validation or fulfillment.

THE POWER OF SELF-RESPECT

When people are secure in their self-respect, it doesn't matter so much what other people think. In a series of experiments, Professors David de Cremer and Tom Tyler found that respect communicates important information about where a person stands. *Am I in or am I out? Am I important, or could people care less about me? Where do I fit in the pecking order?* De Cremer and Tyler found the degree of how respectful we feel others' treatment of us to be influences how worthy and recognized we feel.[6] Our perception of who we are is affected by how we're treated. That determination goes on to influence the number of positive emotions we experience, how cooperative we are, and our willingness to trust others.

In one experiment using student volunteers, the researchers asked the students to sit at computers, where they were told they were being randomly placed in groups and given tasks to perform. First, the volunteers were given a scenario describing a survival situation and asked to rank the fifteen things that would be most important to their survival. Then, while waiting to be placed in a group, the participants were asked to recall a situation where they had been either excluded or included in a group and then write it down.

The test subjects then received a note from the other group members that either communicated respect ("We think your order is very much in line with ours and that we share the same values. Your responses will be helpful to the group.") or disrespect ("We think your order is not in line with ours and you endorse other values than we do. We will not use your responses."). The subjects were then asked a series of questions that determined how much they felt respected and the extent to which they wanted to leave the group. Predictably, the people who felt disrespected were more willing to leave the group. The study also found that for those individuals with a psychological need to belong to a group, respect was very important, but not for those who had a strong sense of self, for whom group membership was unimportant.

People who need to belong to a group react significantly to variations in respect and are much more sensitive to nuance. Those who care a lot about their reputations react strongly to how they are treated. Researchers have found a connection between self-respect and concern for reputation and the need for respect. Respect mattered a lot to those with a high need to belong. Altogether, de Cremer and Tyler report their experiments "consistently show that respect from others influenced self-respect." The stronger your own sense of who you are, the less impact the acts of others have. Or as the researchers put it, "When people's social identities are clear to them they are less influenced by . . . the respect of others."[7]

If you're just bursting with self-confidence, you might be annoyed if someone treats you disrespectfully, but you won't be adversely impacted. But what if you are not brimming with confidence? A lack of self-respect can be destructive.

> The theatre is so endlessly fascinating because it's so accidental. It's so much like life.
> —ARTHUR MILLER

THE PROTECTIVE POWER OF SELF-RESPECT

There are few places where one feels completely and totally at ease. But Lynn Ann Smith is one of the lucky people who has such a place: in front of a class. Whether she is working one-on-one with a child or up late writing lesson plans, the college junior is never happier than when she is teaching. Last spring, she had her first chance to student teach in a real classroom while at the same time privately tutoring high school students in math and English. It was a stressful and hectic time in the coed's life, but her teaching commitments were not the source of the stress. It was her abusive boyfriend.

Along with student teaching, tutor sessions, regular classes, and homework, Lynn Ann was also fitting in twice a week counseling sessions to deal with the trauma of being beaten up by her boyfriend. She'd heard the FBI statistic: that every fifteen seconds in America a woman is battered by the man she loves. She just never imagined it would apply to her.

Thank goodness a neighbor heard what was going on and immediately called the police. Lynn Ann had a bloody nose, a busted lip, and a black eye. It could have been so much worse.

"I will forever be grateful to that woman," says Lynn Ann's father. "I know we can't put our children in a bubble and protect them, but this has been so scary. I go to sleep at night with the telephone number of the state police and campus police on my nightstand." Lynn Ann's parents had never been impressed with the boyfriend, but they never dreamed he could be abusive. He was someone she met at school a year earlier. When university officials were notified of the attack by police, he was arrested and later expelled from school. The court case is still pending.

For Lynn Ann, the official business was the easy stuff. It was what was going on in her head that was hard. How could he have hit her? What had she done to deserve this? Why was she such a horrible judge of character? Could she trust herself to pick a nice boyfriend next time? Could she ever trust a guy to not hit her again? What would happen if she ran into her old boyfriend? After all, he only lived a couple of miles away from campus.

The counseling sessions were a godsend for Lynn Ann. Her counselor helped her understand the dynamics of domestic abuse. She learned just how frequent abuse can be, that one in every four American women is abused at some point in her life and that women in her age group (twenty to twenty-four) are at greatest risk.[8] She learned that she had done nothing wrong. Most importantly, after learning the dynamics of domestic violence, she realized he was the one with issues, not her.

Looking back, Lynn Ann's family is still horrified their daughter was harmed but grateful there was so much going on with their daughter's educational life at the time. "She absorbed herself in all of her teaching responsibilities and that helped her get through all of this," her father says. The student teaching was a needed distraction from the shock and hurt of the attack. When Lynn Ann was in front of a class, she *was* a teacher. The only thing on her mind was how great it was to see those eager little faces looking back at her, knowing she was getting her class excited about learning. At night it was different. Lynn Ann's sleep was interrupted by nightmares and flashbacks.

But the nightmares became less frequent and the flashbacks less frightening as Lynn Ann's twin therapies of teaching and counseling worked their magic. The smiles of the youngsters she saw in class helped erase the pain of the attack. The handwritten thank-you notes her kids made at the end of the term helped rebuild some of the self-esteem chipped away by her ex-boyfriend's cruel comments. Her dad is delighted at the progress but still protectively cautious, as any father would be. "All in all, she is showing great resiliency, but we know this is still a long road for her," he says. "Still, I worry he will reach out to her again one day."

What happened to Lynn Ann, sadly, happens much earlier for some kids. Kids as young as ages thirteen to eighteen face serious pressures in relationships. One in five *teens* in a serious relationship says they have been hit, slapped, or pushed by a partner. One in four teens in a serious relationship says that sex is expected from them. Almost two-thirds (64 percent) said they've had a jealous boyfriend or girlfriend ask where they were all the time.[9] Experts on domestic violence say the blows only come after repeated verbal abuse has diminished a victim's self-esteem. The Power of Self-Respect can be protective.

Self-Respect and Teens

Some kids lack self-respect because they've never been told what it takes to get it. General Colin Powell doesn't mince words in spelling out what young people need to do to earn respect today: "Pull your pants up. Straighten yourself out. Stand up tall. Mind your manners. Mind your teachers. And apply yourself."[10] The former U.S. Secretary of State is the founding chair of America's Promise, a partnership focusing on the well-being of American youth. He says, "We have expectations of you. Don't tell us you're not going to meet our expectations of you. We didn't come to this country as immigrants so you could put something up your nose or so you could fail to get an education or that you can shame us. Go get an education. Graduate from high school. And then you're going to college, whether you like it or not." General Powell has no problem telling teens what's needed to develop self-respect.

As children move into adolescence, their sense of self-worth becomes increasingly connected to their sense of self-image. When the teenage years commence, children begin that age-old task of separating themselves from their parents. Their music differs. The mothers of a generation ago were horrified by the rock lyrics of the sixties and seventies, just as parents today are not too fond of the rap music on their kids' iPods. The ragged jeans and tie-dye shirts of back then are today's teens' baggy pants. Kids demand more independence beginning with walking home from school and going to the movies by themselves. The daughter who used to share everything with her mom no longer does.

At the same time, kids begin to develop a social network. Child psychiatrist Dr. Harold Koplewicz says in seventh or eighth grade, children begin to form deep friendships with other youngsters based on common interests. Boys tend to hang out with kids from their sports teams or, for more studious types, kids who share an academic interest. While girls, he says, may group by sport or affinity for a school subject; the pretty girls may even pal up with the other pretty girls. Koplewicz says that initial common interest is the starting point for a relationship of respect. *Since you are a good lacrosse player and I play lacrosse too, we can be friends,* the thinking might go for a boy. Later when the pal who feels safe in the friendship admits he's not so smart in math, Dr. Koplewicz says the friend will not ridicule him, and he might even be extra respectful and offer to help him out with the subject.

SELF-RESPECT AND GROUP BEHAVIOR

In their study on the role respect plays in groups, professors David de Cremer and Tom Tyler found that respect matters because it communicates information relevant to people's identities. Respect is linked to issues of self-worth, recognition, and inclusion. The more people draw their sense of self-identity from a group, the more strongly influenced they are by whether members of the group treat them with respect. If a child is rejected by the person he thought was his friend or a group he thought he was a part of, it chips away at his sense of self. "Maybe they don't like me after all. Maybe I don't really fit in," he will say to himself. As de Cremer and Tyler put it, "Respect matters because it communicates information relevant to people's identity concerns: 'Do I belong, and where do I stand?'"[11]

For kids without a strong sense of who they are, that overarching question, "Where do I fit in?" can prompt some teens to engage in some activities too soon, some things that are dangerous or have lifelong consequences. Five thousand people under age twenty-one die each year from causes related to underage drinking.[12] You may be stunned to hear how soon it begins. Forty-one percent of eighth graders, 63 percent of tenth graders, and 75 percent of twelfth graders have tried drinking alcohol.[13] Alcohol is often a factor in sexual activity, and it's clear not all sexually active teens are taking sensible precautions. Twenty-six percent of young women between fourteen and nineteen are estimated to be infected with a common sexually transmitted disease.[14]

Bombarded by messages that "thin is in," both boys and girls often suffer from poor body image. The number one wish for girls eleven to seventeen is to be thinner,[15] while boys are busy working out. Those who work out every day to lose weight are twice as likely to experiment with tobacco.[16] Suicide is the third leading cause of death for teens in America.[17] As we saw in chapter 3, bullying is one reason—but it's not the only one.

Here's where self-respect comes in. Researchers' results consistently underscore that respect received from others influenced one's reported self-respect. The more a person cared about how other people viewed him, the more strongly he reacted to feeling rejected or disrespected. Conversely, the person whose sense of self was secure wasn't as influenced by the degree of respect he received. The challenges kids face today are daunting. Add to the list the pressures of juggling grades, a part-time job, the stress of applying to college (and then financing it once you get in), and you get the picture.

THE POWER OF RESPECT

Self-respect can protect us from society's pressures.

Self-respect can function like a Kevlar vest against the pressures of our stress-filled lives—if we have a strong sense of who we are and if we like who we are. How critical is it that parents help foster a strong sense of self for their adolescent children?

Teens need every ounce of self-respect and confidence they can muster to negotiate the treacherous waters of adolescence. Parents can help and children want them to. Kids are eager for their parents to play a role in their lives. In a survey of more than twenty-seven hundred teenagers, most adolescents say the relationship they have with their parents makes them feel good (82 percent). They feel respected by their parents (68 percent) and close to them as well (60 percent).[18]

Parents can use that goodwill by serving as the sounding board their children need as they make choices and by encouraging their kids to develop a talent or skill that helps bolster their child's self-respect.

THE POWER OF RESPECT
Parents can help kids develop a sense of self-respect.

RESPECT IS A WAY OF CARING

Nowhere is the uplifting Power of Self-Respect more apparent than in the story of Ashley Lebovitz. She's a twelve-year-old girl who had no friends. Her mother, Lou Ann, described how it slowly dawned on her that her little girl was terribly isolated. "I can remember thinking that she was just having a bad day the first time I saw her sitting in the cafeteria all by herself. As I went back to see her at lunch a few more times, I realized that every day was the same for her—she would sit by herself with no one to talk to. I couldn't understand how, in a crowded lunchroom crammed with hundreds of middle school kids, Ashley could be completely alone."

Her mother continued, "Observing Ashley at lunch was agonizing for me. She didn't look down, act mad, or seem embarrassed being by herself. She searched and peered at the other kids, with her eyes looking around for any kind of faint glance or contact from anyone. Most middle school students would have just 'acted cool' in a situation like hers, but not Ashley. Being cool was something she didn't understand." Why? Well, Lou Ann explained, Ashley has Down syndrome.

Each day in her innocent, hopeful, yet genuine way, Ashley spent lunch period looking for a friend.

No friends ever materialized at lunch, so Ashley tried a different way to find one. She pulled out the school directory and started dialing. Lou Ann described the Saturday morning ritual. "She'd sit on the floor, phone in one hand, her finger guiding her way through the names, and she would dial the numbers. At first, she would cheerfully leave a message to 'call me back' and move down through the letters of the alphabet. I would try to explain to her that people were busy and attempt to steer her to other activities with our family. But Ashley was determined to find a friend to play with. Her perseverance sometimes paid off, and she'd be encouraged by having someone come over to play." But as the school year continued, the number of kids who would come over or even return her call faded. One day, Ashley was overwhelmed with hurt and frustration.

"She threw the school directory across the room, her eyes fixed on mine, and Ashley declared with steadfast assurance, 'Nobody likes me, I don't have any friends, and I hate myself!'" her mother related. Lou Ann says her daughter recognized the kids weren't mean or being rude to her. It was worse. She didn't *matter* to the kids. "That split-second moment of realization ignited a mound of unresolved feelings for Ashley," her mom continued. "Our entire family became captured in her terrible, downward emotional spiral of low self-respect for the next year."

Oftentimes when it comes to special needs children, the emphasis is on "needs." Lou Ann decided to put her emphasis on the "specialness" of Ashley's condition. Lou Ann expected she'd run into resistance. "People are quick to negatively judge parents who try to 'fix' their kid's problems. Parents of special needs children can be especially vulnerable to such judgments." Lou Ann knew she couldn't fix the situation and make anyone be Ashley's friend, so she decided to find alternative ways Ashley could have meaningful connections with others, connections that would in turn begin to build Ashley's own sense of respect for herself.

"I strived to take Ashley's life from one of isolation to one of giving. I enrolled her in a new school where her natural gifts of kindness and love of people could be valued. I found a church that was accepting of kids with differences. I looked for ways that Ashley could be a contributing member in her groups versus someone on the receiving side of the giving equation, even if it meant that she did very simple gestures."

Ashley began writing "get well" and "thinking of you" cards to people. She developed an amazing memory of people's birthdays and sent homemade "birthday" cards that people enjoyed receiving. Her mother told me, "Ashley used her unique gift of always seeing the best in people, sending cards to just about anyone that was nice to her. She sent cards to people from all walks of life, including servers at restaurants, her numerous doctors, and the neighborhood dry cleaner attendant. She greeted people at events and she helped a classmate with her chair each day." Slowly, Ashley began to feel the Power of Self-Respect when she recognized that her small gestures of respect and kindness were being appreciated.

Ashley began to gradually return to being the happy and caring girl she used to be. Her mom is quick to point out that she and Ashley weren't trying to force an inclusion agenda on anyone or change the prejudices that had been so hurtful in the past. "I simply changed our efforts from finding individual friends to finding ways for Ashley to contribute to others within large circles of people. I was certain that she needed different people in her world."

> Respect is music the deaf can hear and the blind can see.
>
> —UNKNOWN

Lou Ann says like most challenges in life, she learned some important lessons along the way. "We are often taught that respect is something that you earn, and I still agree with that belief to a certain degree. However, with Ashley I learned that respect is a way of caring. You first need to *give* it to individuals and groups before you can receive it." Lou Ann says it was vital that Ashley be appreciated for *her* efforts and her worth before she could gain the respect of others or feel respect for herself. Ashley's mother continued, "I also learned that it's difficult to respect yourself when someone is unable to value your gifts and when you have to be someone you're not intended to be."

> We all have a need to belong . . . we cannot address this need unless we know who we are and where we want to belong.
>
> —NAOMI ELLEMERS

Anyone who has ever built a house knows demolition is much faster than reconstruction. It has taken a lot of time and energy for Ashley and her family to get back on track. Today, Ashley has great friends and people who respect and care for her; as a result, she respects and cares about herself. Ashley still writes many cards, feels good about the things that she does well, and gives her heart to others unselfishly.

"As corny as it sounds," Lou Ann marveled, "my experience with Ashley has confirmed my belief that one small act of respect can make a big difference in the life of another person. The two-way act of giving and receiving respect will be a lifelong effort, I am sure," she continued, "for I know that I'll have many other challenges with Ashley and my own life along the way." But Lou Ann Lebovitz is now convinced she will have an important tool to use in dealing with those challenges: the Power of Respect.

"I am certain," she said, "that whatever opportunities or obstacles that I face, respect is an important gift that I should strive to graciously offer and accept throughout my life."

SELF-RESPECT HELPS YOU
FIND THE BEST ENVIRONMENT

We've all heard the expression "You grow where you're planted." But wouldn't it make the most sense to be planted in an environment that is ideal for your existence? That's what Lou Ann Lebovitz did by putting her special needs daughter in an environment where her natural inclination to be kind would be appreciated. You wouldn't plant an exotic orchid in the woods of Minnesota, and a mountain azalea bush wouldn't last very long in the sandy soils of south Florida. Gardeners study the peculiarities of various cultivars of plants and select only those varieties best suited for the landscape. So what's the best environment for you?

The German philosopher Goethe said, "It is only when we trust ourselves that we truly know how to live." But to do that, you have to be able to answer this question: "Who am I?" It may be one of the most important questions you will ever ask, and the SRI report you did earlier will help you answer it.

THE POWER OF RESPECT
*One of the most important questions
you will ever ask is,"Who am I?"*

What's next? You've tallied up the qualities that you value in yourself. You've estimated how strong you are in each of those traits. These are two important steps toward building your self-respect because you now have a realistic assessment of who you are. The next challenge is *acceptance*. Respect isn't about change and what might be. It's about accepting things as they are. That doesn't mean a defeatist attitude, a resignation to the status quo. On the contrary, it may be that one of the qualities you respect about yourself is your drive and initiative to facilitate change at your business or in your own life.

> He that respects himself is safe from others; he wears a coat of mail that no one can pierce.
> —HENRY WADSWORTH LONGFELLOW

Self-respect acts like a shield to keep real and imagined insults from hurting. It is a leveling agent to keep your emotions from going into overdrive during disappointments. When J.R. Martinez accepted his injured physique and decided it would not define who he was, he began to experience successes he could have never imagined. A soap opera actor? That was never in his thinking. When Ashley Lebovitz's self-respect was bolstered by the delight shown by the recipients of her cards, her world became happier and a little larger. Thanks to a suggestion of a family friend, she and her family are now considering how they might share Ashley's newfound confidence with other special needs kids. They just may go into the greeting card business!

Self-respect that is grounded on a considered assessment like the SRI is not unrealistic head-in-the-clouds silliness but a strong base from which to go forward. It's belief in yourself that is based on the facts. The greater your acceptance of yourself, the less you are impacted by the perceptions of others. The Power of Respect acts as a buffer between disappointments and rejection and damaging blows to your self-confidence.

THE POWER OF RESPECT
The more you accept yourself,
the less others' perceptions matter.

SELF-RESPECT CAN GET YOU THE JOB

Self-respect can also get you the job, even when the odds are against you.

PartsSource CEO Ray Dalton has had a lot of people coming to the door of the medical repair parts supplier looking for work. Located in Ohio, it's not far from a number of automotive-related businesses that have had severe cutbacks because of the well-known problems in that industry. When he's available, Dalton likes to sit in on the interviews. He told me that one recent applicant really stood out.

"He got the job because when this guy walks into the room, you just feel better," Dalton gushed. "Obviously the guy was experiencing challenges because he was out looking for work during a time when jobs are tough to find. But if he was feeling down about himself or his situation, he kept that well hidden." Dalton continued, "He was friendly and informative and told us what was going on. He's only been with the company three or four months, but he's doing great."

Another interviewee in a similar situation with PartsSource didn't make the cut because he didn't have the Power of Respect working for him. "This person might be the nicest person in the world," Dalton said, "but he just depressed you. I told him, 'I am not here to criticize you, but you are not convincing me that you even believe you can do this job. You've got to sit up, you've got to act like you want this job.' He said, 'Well, I've been out of work for four months. It's a tough economy.' I said, 'Well, you'll be out of work for four more months if you don't come around! You're talking to the CEO here, so impress me. What difference could you make here at this company?' He said, 'Well, I'm not sure I could.' I said, 'Then I think you need to go figure out where you can.'"

Dalton knew what the interviewee's problem was. He said, "You have to develop self-respect. It starts at home with the spouse or family being an encourager and you saying, 'I *am* going to make a difference.' Just because your company downsized and you were laid off doesn't change your value to your family or your community or your church. There has been an economic shift, and you just have to stop in your tracks and realize that. People who have lost their jobs are just as valuable as people. You have to say, 'I am going to slug it out every single day just like I did in the beginning. But I am okay.'"

> I think somehow we learn who we really are and then live with that decision.
>
> —ELEANOR ROOSEVELT

People who have self-respect like themselves. They're aware of their strengths and weaknesses and are pleased with the total package. Small failures won't be destabilizing because they don't change the overall opinion they have of themselves.

WAYS TO DEVELOP SELF-RESPECT

How can you generate the Power of Self-Respect in your own life? Here is a brief list of some simple ways you can develop self-respect:

- *Develop the qualities you admire in others.* Get outside of yourself. Try volunteering your time at a charitable organization, coach your kid's soccer team, bring meals to shut-ins who can't get to a store. Volunteering is an others-focused activity that can generate an upward spiral of positive emotions, counteracting some of the negativity. Your SRI can be a big help here.
- *Eliminate judgmental language from your vocabulary.* Don't tell yourself you're "dumb" or "stupid." Everyone makes mistakes. Successful people just make more of them. Vow to do it better next time.
- *Have a positive attitude.* If you are a dishwasher, be the best dishwasher there is. If you are a shoe salesman, be the most helpful salesman retailing has ever known. There is honor in honest work, no matter what the job.
- *Dress the way you want to be seen.* When people have lost their sense of self, sometimes they also lose the drive to make the slightest extra effort. Looking the part you want to play can sometimes be the subtle push in the right direction one needs.
- *Get active.* Do something physical with tangible results. Clean a closet, jog around the block, wash the car. Focusing on another activity prevents you from obsessing over the defeat that's left you reeling.
- *Eat properly.* Burying your troubles in a pint of ice cream won't make your troubles go away and only makes you mad at yourself later. As you've learned, praise the positive. When you resist that bag of chips and head for carrot sticks instead, congratulate yourself on that fine display of willpower.
- *Eliminate toxic people from your life.* We all know people who always seem to find a way to bring us down. Keep

your exposure to these people to a minimum. Surround yourself with those kinds of people who just seem to brighten a room by their presence.

Self-respect is a quality that you can cultivate. It is not dependent on the actions or approval of anyone else. Because you define what is worthy of being respected, you have the unlimited ability to achieve it in your own life. Once you find it, it's like a Fourth of July firecracker that just keeps whizzing toward the heavens. It ignites what psychologists call an "upward spiral"—an ever-rising, ever-replenishing feeling of goodwill. The exponential quality of self-respect is such that once you find one thing you admire about yourself, it enables you to find another and then another.

THE POWER OF RESPECT
Self-respect helps people feel valuable, no matter what their circumstances.

As young Ashley Lebovitz discovered, doing nice things for others made her feel good. That encouraged her to send more thoughtful cards, which had her feeling more proud and others noticing what a nice child she was. She was respected.

J.R. Martinez realized he had a message of hope to share. The more he talked about overcoming adversity, the more confident he became. That confidence is what took his message from a high school gym in north Georgia to the studios of one of the most popular daytime dramas on television. His service to his country would also have earned him respect from others. Now J.R. is able to give respect to himself.

Self-Respect Reminders

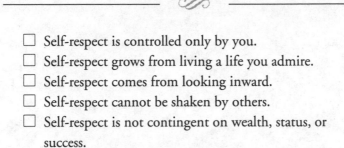

- ☐ Self-respect is controlled only by you.
- ☐ Self-respect grows from living a life you admire.
- ☐ Self-respect comes from looking inward.
- ☐ Self-respect cannot be shaken by others.
- ☐ Self-respect is not contingent on wealth, status, or success.

Conclusion

I wasn't quite sure what I would discover when I began this investigation of the Power of Respect. I'd been raised to believe that you get what you give, to respect your elders, to let others go first, and to treat people the way you'd like them to treat you. I had no idea those simple gestures of decency could yield such dramatic results. Now that I've seen the research done by some of the greatest minds in the field, I am stunned to see the impact of being respected and giving respect. I am also mystified. Why *wouldn't* someone want to put it to work?

If you run a business, why wouldn't you want your employees to be more creative, to be more loyal, to give that little extra to their job—especially when all it takes to encourage it is to let people do their jobs with a little acknowledgment of what they do and recognition of their efforts and successes?

If you're in a relationship, why wouldn't you want to make the bonds of your connection stronger, when all it takes is a little conversation to see what the other person needs—as well as occasionally thanking *them* for the consideration they give you?

If you're a parent, why wouldn't you help your children become confident in who they are and be able to stand up for themselves?

All it takes is asking your children what *they* think, letting them share *their* opinions, and maybe helping them develop a special skill or two they can feel good about.

If you're a teacher, wouldn't you want to be in a school where kids and teachers care about learning and administrators spend most of their time facilitating that, instead of handling disciplinary issues? All it takes is everyone being on the same page about the kind of supportive, encouraging environment you'd like your school to be.

If you lead a group of people, whether it's a scout troop, the garden club, or just a bunch of friends who do potlucks on Saturday night, wouldn't it be great to decide things without so much back and forth? All it takes is letting people feel their opinions matter.

And best of all—it's free. It is not an overstatement to say the Power of Respect may be one of the most forgotten yet potent forces for good. And it doesn't cost a penny!

Consideration, deference, and inclusiveness require nothing but a respectful mind-set. What they return is priceless.

Values in Action— Strengths of Character

Strengths of Wisdom and Knowledge
- Creativity
- Curiosity
- Judgment and open-mindedness
- Love of learning
- Perspective (wisdom)

Strengths of Courage
- Bravery (valor)
- Perseverance (persistence, industriousness)
- Honesty (authenticity, integrity)
- Zest (vitality, enthusiasm, vigor, energy)

Strengths of Humanity
- Capacity to love and be loved
- Kindness (generosity, nurturance, care, compassion, altruistic love, "niceness")

- Social intelligence (emotional intelligence, personal intelligence)

Strengths of Justice
- Teamwork (citizenship, social responsibility, loyalty)
- Fairness
- Leadership

Strengths of Temperance
- Forgiveness and mercy
- Modesty and humility
- Prudence
- Self-regulation (self-control)

Strengths of Transcendence
- Appreciation of beauty and excellence (awe, wonder, elevation)
- Gratitude
- Hope (optimism, future-mindedness, future orientation)
- Humor (playfulness)
- Religiousness and spirituality (faith, sense of purpose)[1]

Notes

Chapter 1: The Most Forgotten Element of Success

1. See Matthew 7:12.
2. See Matthew 22:36–40.
3. Ryne Sandberg, Baseball Hall of Fame induction speech, July 31, 2005. Text available at http://www.cubsnet.com/node/526. Accessed May 29, 2009.
4. Rick Reilly, "Coach John Wooden: A Paragon Rising Above the Madness," *Sports Illustrated*, available at http://tinyurl.com/qwvjm2. Accessed May 29, 2009.
5. Sonia Alleyne, "Oprah Means Business," *Black Enterprise*, June 2008, 117–22.
6. *Inside Edition*, March 9, 2006.
7. For more about the Foundation for Hospital Art, see www.hospitalart.com.
8. John Feight, interview by author, February 19, 2009.
9. *Inside Edition*, May 20, 2008.
10. *Inside Edition*, November 11, 2008.
11. *Inside Edition*, February 13, 2008.
12. Fort Pierce (Florida) Police Department Report, February 28, 2009.

13. Mallory Simon, "My Bullied Son's Last Day on Earth," CNN.com, April 25, 2009.

14. Fox Butterfield, "Man Convicted in Fatal Beating in Dispute at Son's Hockey Game," *New York Times,* January 12, 2002.

15. Steamboat Springs, CO, Police Department report, January 3, 2009.

16. *Aggravating Circumstances: A Status Report on Rudeness in America*—national survey conducted by Public Agenda (2002). Available at www.publicagenda.org.

17. Ibid.

18. Ibid.

19. Ibid.

20. Jerry Wexler, "Aretha Franklin," *Rolling Stone,* April 15, 2004.

21. *The American Heritage Dictionary of the English Language,* 4th ed. (New York: Houghton Mifflin, 2009), s.v. "respect."

22. *Aggravating Circumstances,* Public Agenda, 2002.

23. *Teaching Interrupted.* A nationwide study prepared by Public Agenda for Common Good (2004).

24. Corporate Leavers Survey. Level Playing Field Institute (2007).

25. Deborah Norville, *Thank You Power: Making the Science of Gratitude Work for You* (Nashville: Thomas Nelson, 2007).

Chapter 2: It All Starts at Home

1. Peter Applebome, "Atwitter About a Mom in Scarsdale," *New York Times,* April 22, 2009.

2. Bozell Worldwide/ *U.S. News & World Report,* "Civility in America Study," 1999.

3. Interview with David Gergen, *The NewsHour with Jim Lehrer,* August 5, 1998.

4. Author's interview with Dr. Harold Koplewicz. For more information about Dr. Koplewicz and the New York University Child Study Center, see www.aboutourkids.org.

5. Author's interview with Dr. Mary Pulido. For more information about Dr. Pulido and the New York Society for the Prevention of Cruelty to Children, see www.nyspcc.org.

6. Louis Harris Associates, *Reader's Digest* poll of 2,000 high school seniors (1994).

7. B. S. Bowden and J. M. Zeisz, "Supper's on! Adolescent adjustment and frequency of family mealtimes." Paper presented at the 105th Annual Meeting of the American Psychological Association, Chicago, IL, August 15, 1997.

8. Author's interview with Jacques Savarèse.

9. R. F. Baumeister, C. Finkenauer, and K. D. Vohs, "Bad is stronger than good," *Review of General Psychology,* vol. 5, no. 4 (2001): 323–70.

10. J. H. Corpus, C. M. Ogle, K. E. Love-Geiger, "The Effects of Social-Comparison Versus Mastery Praise on Children's Intrinsic Motivation," *Motivation & Emotion,* 30 (2006): 335–45.

11. Ibid., 340.

12. N. Gallagher, "Effects of parent-child interaction therapy on young children with disruptive behavior disorders," *Bridges,* vol. 1, no. 7 (2003).

13. Teens Today Driving Study for Liberty Mutual and SADD (Students Against Destructive Decisions), 2006.

Chapter 3: The Glue That Keeps Us Together

1. Lee and Bob Woodruff, *In An Instant* (New York: Random House, 2007).

2. For more information on the Bob Woodruff Foundation, see www.ReMind.org.

3. Centers for Disease Control, National Vital Statistics Report, vol. 52, 22, June 10, 2004.

4. "Runaway mom goes back to Pa. to face charges," *Today* People, May 29, 2009, www.msnbc.msn.com/id/30996217.

5. For more information on Michele Weiner-Davis, see www.divorcebusting.com.

6. C. D. Batson, "Why act for the public good? Four answers," *Journal of Personality and Social Psychology* 20 (1994): 603–10.

7. M. H. Cantor, "Neighbors and Friends: An Overlooked Resource in the Informal Support System," *Research on Aging,* vol. 1, no. 4 (1979): 434–63; R. C. Mannell, J. Zuzanek, R. Larson, "Leisure states and 'flow' experiences: Testing perceived freedom and intrinsic motivation hypotheses," *Journal of Leisure Research,* vol. 20 (4) (1988): 289–304.

8. T. C. Antonucci and H. Akiyama, "Social relationships and aging well," *Generations*, XV (1) (1990): 39–44.

9. B. Hess and B. Soldo, "Husband and wife networks," in W. J. Sauer and R. T. Coward (eds.), *Social support networks and the care of the elderly: Theory, research, and practice* (New York: Springer, 1985), 67–92.

10. D. de Cremer and T. R. Tyler, "Am I respected or not?: Inclusion and reputation as issues in group membership," *Social Justice Research* 18, 2 (2005): 121–53.

11. Gallup Poll, Q12 Survey, *Gallup Management Journal*, May 26, 1999.

12. K. Jehn and P. Shah, "Interpersonal relationships and task performance: An examination of mediating processes in friendship and acquaintance groups," *Journal of Personality and Social Psychology* 72, 4 (1997): 775–90.

13. Harris Interactive Poll, "Doctors' Interpersonal Skills Valued More than Their Training or Being Up-to-Date," October 1, 2004.

14. CDC 1998 as reported in "Life's First Crossroad: Tweens make choices that affect their lives forever" (May 2000).

15. Indicators of School Crime and Safety 2008, National Center for Education Statistics.

16. www.ryanpatrickhalligan.com.

17. D. Olweus, "Bully/victim problems among schoolchildren: Long-term consequences and an effective intervention program," quoted in S. Hodgins, *Mental Disorder and Crime* (Thousand Oaks, CA: Sage Publications, 1993), 317–49.

18. T. R. Nansel, M. Overpeck, R. S. Pilla, W. J. Ruan, B. Simons-Morton, and P. Scheidt, "Bullying behaviors among U.S. youth: Prevalence and association with psychosocial adjustment," *Journal of the American Medical Association* 285, 16 (2001).

19. Centers for Disease Control and Prevention.

20. A. D. Pellegrini, M. Bartini, and F. Brooks, "School bullies, victims, and aggressive victims: Factors relating to group affiliation and victimization in early adolescence," *Journal of Educational Psychology* 9, 2 (1999): 216–24.

21. P. C. Rodkin, T. W. Farmer, R. Pearl, and R. Van Acker, "Heterogeneity of popular boys: Antisocial and prosocial configurations," *Developmental Psychology* 36, 1 (2000): 14–24.

22. M. Fekkes, F. Pijpersand, and S. Verloove-Vanhorick, "Bullying: Who does what, when, and where? Involvement of children, teachers, and parents in bullying behavior," *Health Education Research* 20 (2005): 81–91.

23. K. Rigby, *Bullying in Schools: and What to Do About It* (London: Jessica Kingsley Publishers, 1994).

24. Norton Online Living Report (June 2008), www.nortononlineliving.com/documents/NOLR_Report_09.pdf.

25. Louisiana Youth Suicide Prevention Task Force, S.T.A.R. 2001 Report, Louisiana Adolescent Health Initiative.

26. A. M. Horne, J. L. Stoddard, and C. D. Bell, "Group approaches to reducing aggression and bullying in school," *Group Dynamics: Theory, Research, and Practice* 11, 4 (2007): 262–71.

27. Z. Schechtman and M. Ben-David, "Individual and group psychotherapy of childhood aggression: A comparison of outcomes and processes," *Group Dynamics: Theory, Research, and Practice* 3 (1999): 263–74.

28. S. Melman, S. G. Little, and K. A. Akin-Little, "Adolescent overscheduling: The relationship between levels of participation in scheduled activities and self-reported clinical symptomology," *High School Journal* 90 (2007): 18–30.

29. Ibid.

30. A. E. Field, S. B. Austin, C. A. Camargo Jr, C. B. Taylor, R. H. Striegel-Moore, K. J. Loud, and G. A. Colditz, "Exposure to the Mass Media, Body Shape Concerns, and Use of Supplements to Improve Weight and Shape Among Male and Female Adolescents," *Pediatrics*, August 1, 2005, 116 (2): e214–20.

31. M. A. Bisson and T. R. Levine, "Negotiating a friends with benefits relationship," *Archives of Sexual Behavior* 38 (2009): 66–73.

32. G. M. Wingwood, R. J. DiClemente, J. M. Bernhardt, K. Harrington, S. L. Davies, A. Robillard, and E. W. Hook III, "A prospective study of exposure to rap music videos and African-American female adolescents' health," *American Journal of Public Health* 93, 3, 437–439 (March 2003).

33. "This Is My Reality: The Price of Sex," a study conducted by MEE for California Endowment and the Ford Foundation, 2004.

Chapter 4: Taming the Blackboard Jungle

1. R. L. Curwin and A. Mendler, "Discipline with Dignity," Association for Supervision and Curriculum Development, 1988.
2. T. H. Benton, "No Respect," *Chronicle of Higher Education*, vol. 50, no. 18 (2004).
3. Ibid.
4. Ibid.
5. Wauwatosa, WI, Police Department, February, 11, 2009.
6. Seventy-three percent of teachers and 68 percent of parents agree, "There's disrespect everywhere in our culture—kids absorb it and bring it with them to school." *Teaching Interrupted*. A nationwide study prepared by Public Agenda for Common Good (2004).
7. *Teaching Interrupted*, Ibid.
8. National Center for Education Statistics—*Indicators of School Crime and Safety* (December 2007).
9. S. L. Wessler, "Rebuilding classroom relationships: It's hard to learn when you're scared," *Educational Leadership*, vol. 61, no. 1 (2003).
10. K. Futernick, *A Possible Dream: Retaining California teachers so all students can learn* (Sacramento: California State University, 2007).
11. PBIS Maryland Management Team, Update on PBIS Maryland and Collaborative Research Efforts, November 17, 2008.
12. K. Futernick, *A Possible Dream*, Ibid.
13. "Mouth Watch," *People*, September 13, 1999.
14. PBIS Maryland Management Team, Ibid.
15. Ibid.
16. K. Futernick, *A Possible Dream*, Ibid.
17. R. J. Vallerand, M. S. Fortier, and F. Guay, "Self-determination and persistence in a real-life setting: Toward a motivational model of high school dropout," *Journal of Personality and Social Psychology* 72 (1997): 1161–76.
18. E. L. Deci, A. Schwartz, L. Sheinman, and R. M. Ryan, "An instrument to assess adults' orientations toward control versus autonomy with children: Reflections on intrinsic motivation and perceived competence," *Journal of Educational Psychology* 73 (1981): 642–50.

19. R. Koestner, R. M. Ryan, F. Bernieri, and K. Holt, "Setting limits on children's behavior: The differential effects of controlling versus information styles on intrinsic motivation and creativity," *Journal of Personality* 2 (1984): 233–48.

20. B. C. Patrick, E. A. Skinner, and J. P. Connell, "What motivates children's behavior and emotion? Joint effects of perceived control and autonomy in the academic domain," *Journal of Personality and Psychology* 65 (1993): 781–91.

Chapter 5: The Best Business Tool—and It's Free!

1. Peter Georgescu, *The Source of Success* (San Francisco: Jossey-Bass, 2005).

2. According to the company's Web site, www.google.com.

3. Smithsonian Institution Web site. http://invention.smithsonian.org/centerpieces/iap/inventors_fry.html.

4. Deborah Norville, *Thank You Power: Making the Science of Gratitude Work for You* (Nashville: Thomas Nelson, 2007), 34–6.

5. Answers to the quiz: 1. Cheese 2. Power.

6. Development Dimensions International Study (2007).

7. T. A. Judge, A. Erez, and J. E. Bono, "The power of being positive: The relation between positive self-concept and job performance," *Human Performance* 11, 2 (1998): 167–87.

8. T. A. Judge, J. A. LePine, and B. L. Rich, "Loving yourself abundantly: Relationship of the narcissistic personality to self and other perceptions of workplace deviance, leadership, and task and contextual performance," *Journal of Applied Psychology* 91, 4 (2006): 762–76.

9. T. A. Judge, R. F. Piccolo, and R. Ilies, "The forgotten ones? The validity of consideration and initiating structure in leadership research," *Journal of Applied Psychology* 89, 1 (2004): 36–51.

10. Tim Judge, personal e-mail to author.

11. Fast Company 50, 2009. Available at www.fastcompany.com/fast50_09/profile/list/zappos.

12. www.zappos.com.

13. Sirota Survey Intelligence, Respect Related to Employee Retention (2006).

14. Corporate Leaders Survey, Level Playing Field Institute (2007).

15. R. J. Bies and T. R. Tyler, "The 'Litigation Mentality' in organizations: A test of alternative psychological explanations," *Organizational Science* 4, 3 (1993).

16. D. P. Leven, "GM agrees to settle blacks' lawsuit," *New York Times*, February 1, 1989.

17. R. J. Bies and T. R. Tyler, "The 'Litigation Mentality' in Organizations."

18. E. A. Lind, "Litigation and claiming in organizations: Antisocial behavior or quest for justice?" *Antisocial Behavior in Organizations* (Thousand Oaks, CA: Sage Publications, 1997).

19. E. A. Lind, J. Greenberg, K. S. Scott, and T. D. Welchans, "The winding road from employee to complainant: Situational and psychological determinants of wrongful termination claims," *Administrative Science Quarterly* 45 (2000): 557–90.

20. U.S. Labor Department report, May 8, 2009.

21. www.partssource.com.

22. U.S. Labor Department report, May 8, 2009.

23. T. A. Judge, C. J. Thoresen, and V. Pucik, "Managerial coping with organization change: A dispositional perspective," presented at the annual meeting of the Academy Management (August 1996).

24. L. J. Sanna, "Self-efficacy theory: Implications for social facilitation and social loafing," *Journal of Personality and Social Psychology* 62 (1992): 774–86.

25. © 2000–2009 Management Issues Ltd. All rights reserved. www.management-issues.com.

26. T. A. Judge, A. Erez, and J. E. Bono, "The power of being positive," Ibid.

27. A. M. Isen and J. Reeve, "The Influence of Positive Affect on Intrinsic and Extrinsic Motivation: Facilitating Enjoyment of Play, Responsible Work Behavior, and Self-Control," *Motivation and Emotion*, 29, 4 (2005): 297–325.

28. Ibid.

Chapter 6: The Leadership Magnet

1. National Technology Readiness Survey, University of Maryland/ Rockbridge Associates, 2005.

2. J. M. Burns, *Leadership* (New York: Harper & Row, 1978).

3. B. M. Bass, B. J. Avolio, D. I. Jung, and Y. Berson, "Predicting unit performance by assessing transformational and transactional leadership," *Journal of Applied Psychology* 88, 2 (2003): 207–18.

4. B. M. Bass and B. J. Avolio, "Transformational leadership and organizational culture," *Public Administration Quarterly* (Spring 1993): 112–21. See also B. J. Avolio, B. M. Bass, and D. Jung, "Reexamining the components of transformational and transactional leadership using the Multifactor Leadership Questionnaire," *Journal of Occupational and Organizational Psychology* 7 (1999): 441–62.

5. "America's loss of global respect," Survey for Pew Charitable Foundation by Public Agenda, 2008.

6. Inaugural address of President Barack Obama, January 20, 2009.

7. E. A. Lind and T. R. Tyler, *The Social Psychology of Procedural Justice* (New York: Plenum, 1988).

8. D. de Cremer and T. R. Tyler, "The effects of trust in authority and procedural fairness on cooperation," *Journal of Applied Psychology* 92, 3 (2007): 639–49.

9. Ibid., 641.

10. T. R. Tyler, "Social Justice: Outcome and procedure," *International Journal of Psychology* 35, 2 (2000): 117–25.

11. T. R. Tyler and Y. J. Huo, *Trust in the Law: Encouraging Public Cooperation with the Police and Courts* (New York: Russell Sage Foundation, 2002).

12. D. de Cremer and T. R. Tyler, "Managing group behavior: The interplay between procedural justice, sense of self, and cooperating," quoted in M. Zanna, ed., *Advances in Experimental Social Psychology*, 37 (2005): 151–218.

13. C. Peterson and N. Park, "Character strengths in organizations," *Journal of Organizational Behavior* 27, 8 (2006): 1149–54

14. T. M. Amabile and S. J. Kramer, "Inner work life: Understanding the subtext of business performance," *Harvard Business Review* (May 2007): 72–83. See also T. M. Amabile, E. A. Schatzel, G. B. Moneta, and S. J. Kramer, "Leader behaviors and the work environment for creativity: Perceived leader support," *Leadership Quarterly* 15,1 (2004): 5–32.

15. T. M. Amabile, C. N. Hadley, and S. J. Kramer, "Creativity under the gun," *Harvard Business Review* (August 2002): 52–61.

16. D. B. McFarlin, R. F. Baumeister, and J. Blascovich, "On knowing when to quit: Takes failure, self-respect, advice, and nonproductive persistence," *Journal of Personality* 52, 2 (1984): 138–55.

17. L. J. Sanna, "Self-efficacy theory: Implications for social facilitation and social loafing," *Journal of Personality and Social Psychology* 62 (1992): 774–86.

18. H. Sauermann and W. Cohen, *Fire in the Belly? Individuals' motives and innovative performance in startups versus established firms.* Working paper (Durham, NC: Duke University, 2007b).

19. B. Kaye and S. Jordan-Evans, *Engaging the massive middle,* Career Systems International (2007).

20. T. A. Judge, R. F. Piccolo, and R. Ilies, "The forgotten ones? The validity of consideration and initiating structure in leadership research," *Journal of Applied Psychology* 89, 1 (2004): 36–51.

21. B. van Knippenberg and D. van Knippenger, "Leader self-sacrifice and leadership effectiveness: The moderating role of leader prototypicality," *Journal of Applied Psychology* 90, 1 (2005): 25–37.

22. J. B. Fuller, C. E. P. Patterson, K. Hester, and D. Y. Stinger, "A quantitative review of research on charismatic leadership," *Psychological Reports* 78 (1996): 271–87.

Chapter 7: It's on the Inside

1. T. R. Tyler, "Cooperation in organizations: A social identity perspective," quoted in M. A. Hogg and D. J . Terry, eds., *Social Identity Processes in Organizational Contexts* (Philadelphia: Psychology Press, 2001).

2. T. R. Tyler and H. J. Smith, "Justice, social identity, and group processes," quoted in T. R. Tyler, R. M. Kramer, and O. P. John, eds., *The Psychology of the Social Self* (Mahaw, NJ: Erlbaum, 1999).

3. D. de Cremer and T. R. Tyler, "Am I respected or not? Inclusion and reputation as issues in group membership," *Social Justice Research* 18, 2 (2005): 121–55.

4. D. de Cremer, "Respect and cooperation in social dilemmas: The importance of feeling included," *Personality and Social Psychology Bulletin* 28 (2002): 1335–41.

5. T. R. Tyler and S. Blader, *Cooperation in Groups: Procedural Justice, Social Identity, and Behavioral Engagement* (Philadelphia: Psychology Press, 2000).

6. D. de Cremer and T. R. Tyler, "Am I respected or not?" 121–55.

7. Ibid.

8. Patricia Tjaden and Nancy Thoennes, "Extent, nature and consequences of intimate partner violence: Findings from the National Violence Against Women survey," National Institute of Justice and the Centers for Disease Control and Prevention, 2000.

9. Teen Research Unlimited (TRU) survey of 13 to 18 year olds for Liz Claiborne, Inc. (2006).

10. Interview with CNN's Soledad O'Brien, aired March 14, 2009.

11. D. de Cremer and T. R. Tyler, "Am I respected or not?", 121–55.

12. National Institutes of Health Underage Drinking Fact Sheet, July 2007.

13. 2005 National Survey on Drug Use and Health.

14. Centers for Disease Control STD Study, presented March 11, 2008, 2008 National STD Prevention Conference, Chicago, IL.

15. "Facts on Body and Image," Just Think Foundation.

16. A. Marcus, "Body Image Tied to Smoking in Kids," Health Scout, Merck-Medco Managed Care, 1999.

17. Teens Today Survey for Students Against Destructive Decisions, 2008.

18. Ibid.

Appendix: Values in Action—Strengths of Character

1. Christopher Peterson and Martin E. P. Seligman, *Character Strengths and Virtues: A Handbook and Classification* (Oxford University Press and American Psychological Association, 2004). Available at www.viacharacter.org. Also quoted in Deborah Norville, *Thank You Power: Making the Science of Gratitude Work for You* (Nashville: Thomas Nelson, 2007), 147–8.

About the Author

Deborah Norville is the anchor of *Inside Edition*, the nation's top-rated and longest-running syndicated television magazine. The two-time Emmy-Award winner is a summa cum laude graduate of the University of Georgia and began her television career at WAGA-TV in Atlanta while still a college student.

Formerly the co-anchor of NBC's *Today*, Deborah has reported and anchored for WMAQ-TV in Chicago, NBC News, CBS News, and MSNBC and hosted a national radio show for ABC Radio.

Deborah is also a best-selling author. Her titles include *Back on Track*, *I Don't Want to Sleep Tonight*, *I Can Fly*, *Knit with Deborah Norville*, and the *New York Times* bestseller, *Thank You Power*.

Recently, Deborah introduced a line of fine knitting and crochet yarns, tapping into her lifelong passion of knitting and sewing. She and her husband, Karl Wellner, live in New York City with their three children. Deborah can be reached via her Web site: www.dnorville.com.